STAGE PROPERTIES AND HOW TO MAKE THEM

WARREN KENTON

PITMAN, LONDON
DRAMA BOOK SPECIALISTS, NEW YORK

PITMAN PUBLISHING LIMITED
39 Parker Street, London WC2B 5PB

Associated Companies
Copp Clark Limited, Toronto
Pitman Publishing New Zealand Ltd, Wellington
Pitman Publishing Pty Ltd, Melbourne

Published simultaneously in the USA by
Drama Book Specialists, 150 West 52nd Street, New York, NY 10019

First published in Great Britain 1964
Reprinted 1966, 1967, 1971, 1974
Second Edition, published in paperback, 1978

UK ISBN 0 273 01163 4
US ISBN 0 910482 97 7

Reproduced and printed by photolithography and bound in Great Britain at The Pitman Press, Bath

PREFACE

STAGE properties play their part in relation to a theatrical production as a whole by enhancing the effects of words, action and scene. They perform their work by embroidering the illusion evoked on the stage. Skilfully used, they have the power to transform a beggar into a prince, to make a forest rise from the boards, and even stars to fall as from the heavens. The making of stage properties might be called an almost magical craft, for although its influence is felt, it is rarely *observed* except by the people who know the skilled work behind the paper and paste, the wood and wire.

W.K.

To

Browning Hall

CONTENTS

PART I

INTRODUCTORY

If you are designing your own props first try to catch the mood and meaning of the theme of the play. Study as many references as possible about the period and the place in which the action evolves. Decide which are the most characteristically evocative qualities, and, keeping these qualities in your mind, work out your own design.

If, on the other hand, you are following a designer's drawing, try to appreciate his interpretation of the theme. If possible, discuss it with him and do not hesitate to ask for a precise indication of what he wants done. If he is a good designer he will realize the importance of the practical side. Always bear in mind the feel of the thing you are making and use the simplest and most direct method of conveying the essential character of the design. Work at your own speed if possible.

TOOLS AND MATERIALS

Workshop Needs

Space	Sink	Bench
Light	Gas-ring	Large doorway

Carpentry Tools

Vice
Hammer
Saws (tenon, fret)
Screwdrivers (large and small)
Pliers (bull- and long-nose)
Pincers
Tin-snips (shears)
Wheel-brace (set of drills)
Two buckets (glue and water)
Brace (set of drills)
Files (coarse and fine)
Planes (large and small)
Spokeshave
Chisels (set of sizes)
Bradawl
Sharp knife (Stanley)
Sandpaper (coarse and fine)
Glue brush

Specialist Tools

Scissors (large and small)
Needles (for cottons and threads)
Pins and paper-clips
Rulers (inch, foot, yard, six-foot)
Pens and pencils
Protractor
Steel straight-edge
Set-square and T-square
Brushes (full selection)
Compass (small metal, large wood)
Charcoal
Chalk

Carpentry Materials

Pile of timber (all varieties, shapes and sizes)
Plywood (three and six thicknesses)
Skin-ply
Block-board (half-inch)
Hardboard, strawboard
Bamboo (various lengths and thicknesses)
Cane (various lengths and thicknesses)
Poles and dowelling (various lengths and thicknesses)
Broomsticks, lathes
Beading
Nails (selection)
Screws (selection)
Tacks (selection)
Pins (selection)
Nuts and bolts (selection)
Staples (selection)

Property Materials

Boxes of junk (door-handles, bed-springs, old clocks, etc.)
Boxes of rags and canvas
Boxes of newspaper

Wires

Flower wires (thick and thin bundles)
Chicken-wire (inch and half-inch rolls of netting)
Coils of galvanized wire (selection of gauges)
Millinery wire
Copper wire
Brass wire
Fuse wire
Silver wire

Papers

For Papier Mâché

Sugar (strong base covering)
Brown (strong base covering)
Newspaper (general covering and modelling)
Tissue (fine finish)

General Purpose

Tracing, carbon
Cartridge, lining
Card, corrugated

Tapes

Sticky paper (water-dipped)
White self-adhesive cloth
Black self-adhesive cloth
Scotch transparent (self-sticking)
Masking paper (self-sticking)
Wired parcel paper (malleable non-sticking)

Glues

Carpenters' (blocks, sheets, grains)
Bostik (clear spirit adhesive)
Copydex (quick-drying rubber adhesive)
Cow Gum (slow-drying rubber adhesive)
Water paste
Size

Paints, etc.

Pigments (full range of colours)
Emulsion medium (a quick-drying plastic fluid)
Emulsion glaze (as above only richer in shine)
Cellulose high flash varnish
Size
Metal dusts (bronze, silver, etc.)
French polish (shellac)
Dyes (full range of colours)
Methylated spirit (medium for spirit dyes and french enamels)
French enamel varnishes (full range)
Ultra-violet paints (full range)

Modelling

Clay, Plasticine, wax
Plaster of Paris
Petroleum jelly (for greasing moulds and master shapes)
Latex (a rubber fluid that hardens)
Fibreglass, Polystyrene, Vinyl
Modelling tools
Alabastine
Plastic wood
Putty

Cloths

Jap silk
Velvet
Muslin (book muslin, butcher's muslin)
Animal baize
Canvas
Netting
Scrim
Gauze
Bandage
Leather
Felt (fine and coarse, many colours, paper-backed)
Linen (sign-writer's linen, flower-maker's linen)
Sheeting (stiffened and unstiffened)
Buckram

Cloth Stiffeners

Gelatine
Straw stiffener

Anti-fray Materials

Straw stiffeners
Fire-resistant nettings

Metals

Sheet aluminium
Sheet lead
Sheet alloy
Sheet brass
Tube aluminium (various diameters)
Tube iron (various diameters)
Strap iron
Strap brass
Angled irons and plates
Metal discs, wheels, knobs, etc.

Woods
(for specialized work)

Bamboo (rigid)
Cane (pliable)
Balsa (light)
Spruce (tough, light)
Willow canes and rods (very pliable)
Teak (close-grained, strong, heavy)
Oak (close-grained, strong, heavy)

Decorative Accessories

Sequins (all colours and shapes)
Glitter (fine, coarse and all colours)
Cardboard tubes (various diameters)
Gold dust
Bronze dust
Silver dust
Metal foils (all colours)
Paper foils (all colours)
Tissues (all colours)
Cinemoid (all colours)
Gelatine (clear)
Iridescent transparent papers
Gold and silver wires
Hooks
Marbles (all colours)
Shells
Pearls
Pieces of decorative fabric
Coins
Chains
Buttons
Webbing
Leathers
Polythene
Glass jewels
Sweets (wine gums for jewels)
Bottle-tops
Sweet-wrappers
Ropes
Tapes
Cords
Threads
Buckles
Press studs
Hooks and eyes
Beads
Wooden balls (various diameters)
Feathers (all colours and kinds)
Hemp, sisal
Stones (coloured)
Lace
Medals
Braids
Buckram
Elastic
Foam rubber

BOOKS OF REFERENCE

ACCURATE books of reference are most important. Illustrated encyclopedias are useful to give a general survey of a period, but often one needs greater detail. This can usually be obtained with the help of the local public librarian. It is also a good idea to keep a folder for pictures cut from magazines and newspapers; in the course of a year a remarkably wide range of references will be collected.

FIRE-PROOFING

THE law is that all stage settings must be fire-proofed, and this generally includes props. Fire-proofing crystals can be bought ready for use or a solution can be made up from 15 oz of boracic-acid crystals and 10 oz of sodium phosphate in a gallon of water. Be careful how you spray the solution, for colours may run or delicate shapes be damaged.

BASIC TECHNIQUES

In the section that follows an outline is given of basic methods and materials. There are others, but these have proved their worth and are as good as any.

The outline follows the natural order of the construction process, that is, framework, covering, and painting. Detail and decoration are founded upon these basic techniques and the care with which they are applied will determine the durability, quality, and last, but never least, the cost of a given prop.

FRAMEWORK

Woods

The basic material of many props is wood. The reason is that wood is both strong and easy to work. There are many kinds of wood and each has a feature that can be used to advantage, e.g. skin-ply's bendability or balsa's lightness. Learn to select the timber most suitable for the job and design the framework of your object to use the timber's particular quality to the full.

Little need be said about the actual carpentry involved for a competent amateur can deal with most problems. However it is wise to become acquainted with the proprietor of the local woodwork shop, for there band-saws, lathes, power drills, and other machinery for working timber will be available (at a fee) to do the more laborious or excessively difficult jobs.

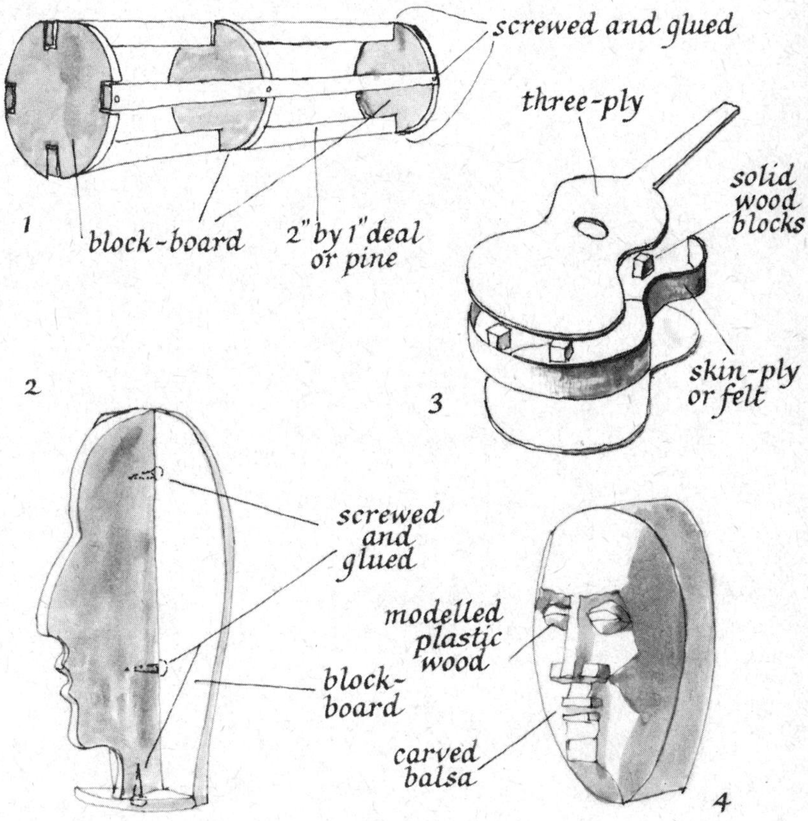

1. General timber constructions: in this example a column or tree
2. Block-board fretted, screwed and glued into base shape for head
3. Ply and skin-ply fretted, cut, glued and pinned into guitar
4. Carved and glued balsa or plastic wood modelled into face

FIGURE 1

FRAMEWORK

Galvanized Wire

Galvanized wire is perhaps as important as wood in this craft of property making, for from it can be made almost any shape to, within certain limits, any size. Its chief virtue lies in its malleability, which gives it an enormous range of uses. Twisted and bent, cross-bound and woven, it can be locked into structures that are both light, strong, and delicate to form the under-shape for papier mâché, paint, and decoration.

Stock, if you can, seven-pound coils of three differing gauges: thick, three-sixteenths of an inch; medium, one-twelfth of an inch; and thin, one-sixteenth of an inch (the measurements are approximate). If a thick gauge is unobtainable, strength can be achieved by binding two or three thinner wires together.

Adhesive tape is used to bind wire, and a cloth-backed variety is the best. Half an inch is a good width and this can always be split into quarter of an inch for the more delicate bindings.

Three methods of taping are shown opposite. There are many others, which will be quickly discovered by experience. Bear in mind always the need to reconcile minimum weight with maximum strength.

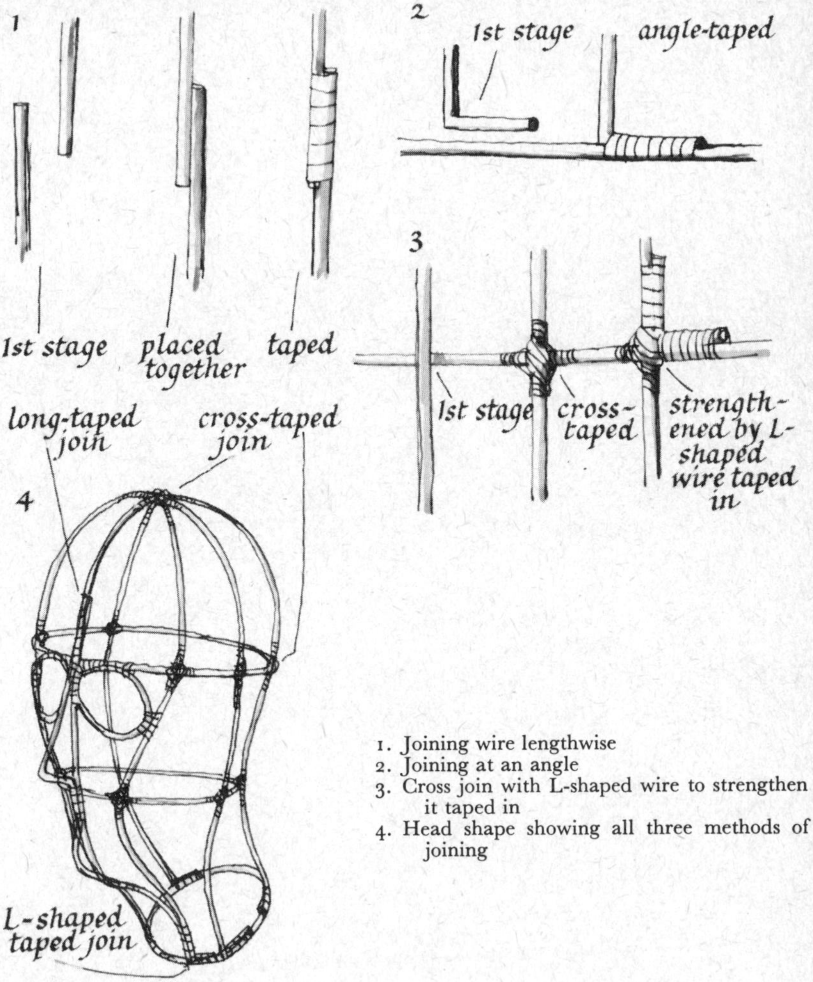

1. Joining wire lengthwise
2. Joining at an angle
3. Cross join with L-shaped wire to strengthen it taped in
4. Head shape showing all three methods of joining

FIGURE 2

FRAMEWORK

Cane

For certain large jobs cane, because of its strength and lightness, is sometimes more suitable than wire. Cane also has the advantage of being decorative in its own right so that it is suitable to use if the object is to have no covering of papier mâché or cloth. It can often be used in conjunction with wire to form the master skeleton of objects for which six thicknesses of wire would obviously be too heavy. In fact, one might say generally that cane comes into its own where the weight of wire cancels out the advantages of its strength.

Cane is shaped and bent by heat, either in steam or over a gas-ring or electric fire. Work patiently, bending the cane gently and firmly, section by section along the length. Be careful not to miss any part or an ugly kink will appear—unless, of course, you want an angle rather than a curve.

Joining is done by the methods illustrated; holes are drilled in the cane, through which wire is looped and twisted. When cane is to be used as a central spine with wires radiating out from it, drill the cane, pierce it and insert the wire into the cane, and bend the wire at right-angles so that one arm of the angle lies along the cane for an inch; tape this arm to the case to secure it (*see* (5) opposite).

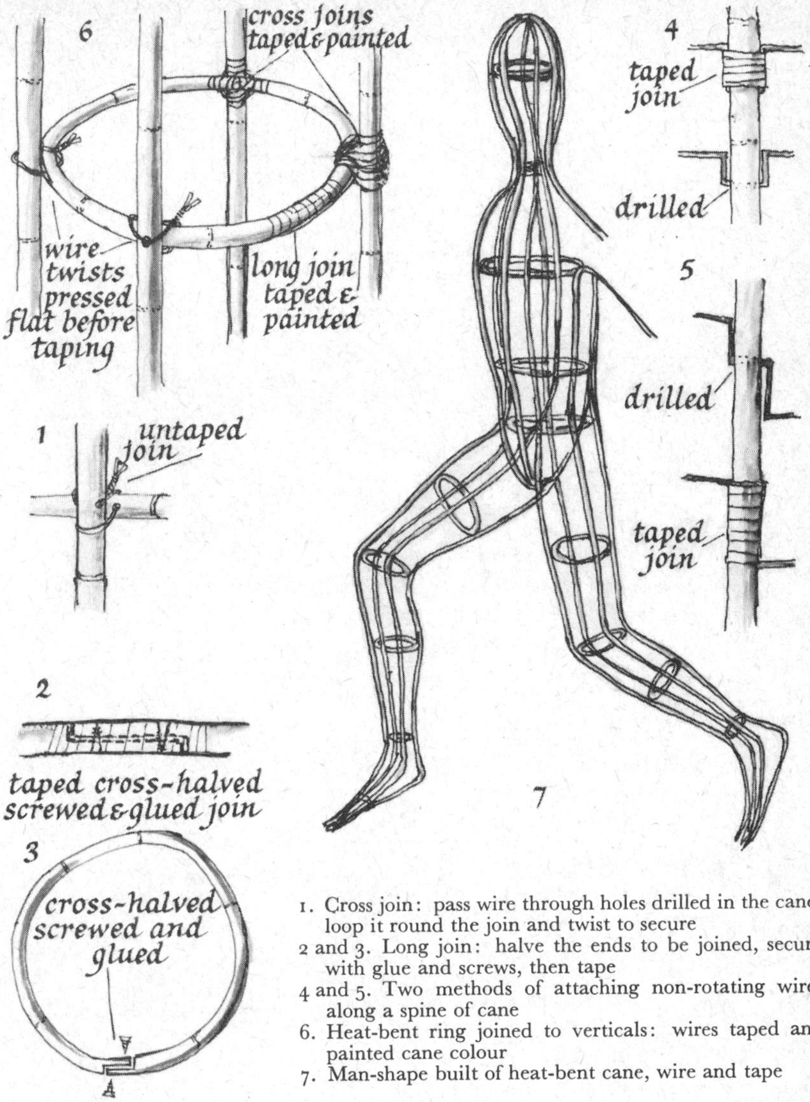

1. Cross join: pass wire through holes drilled in the cane, loop it round the join and twist to secure
2 and 3. Long join: halve the ends to be joined, secure with glue and screws, then tape
4 and 5. Two methods of attaching non-rotating wires along a spine of cane
6. Heat-bent ring joined to verticals: wires taped and painted cane colour
7. Man-shape built of heat-bent cane, wire and tape

FIGURE 3

FRAMEWORK

Chicken-wire

To clothe the main framework and provide a foundation on which to build the papier-mâché covering, chicken-wire is excellent, for it has both strength and malleability. Clipped and roughly shaped, it can be moulded round and over formers to almost any contour. Because of its net-like nature, it can be elongated or contracted in any direction.

Chicken-wire is available in rolls of half-inch or one-inch netting four feet or five feet wide and perhaps thirty feet in length. It may be cut with shears or a big pair of old scissors.

To fix it to wood, staple it using either a hammer or a special canvas staple-gun. To marry one piece of wire to another, interfold the open ends of the wire cells on the cut edge, or sew them together with thin galvanized wire.

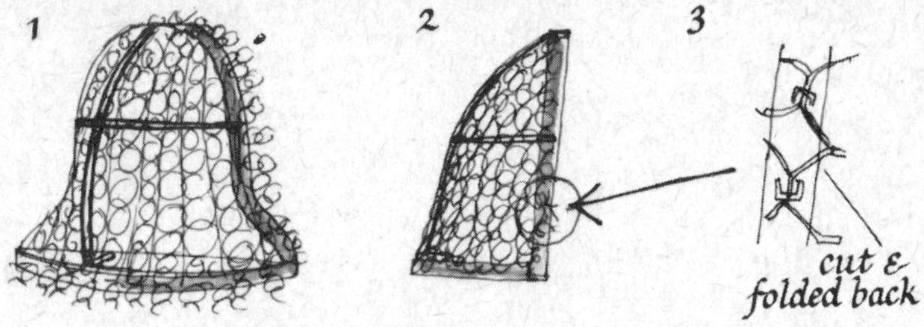

1. Block-board shape with chicken-wire stapled along edges
2. Chicken-wire neatly trimmed flush
3. Detail of stapling

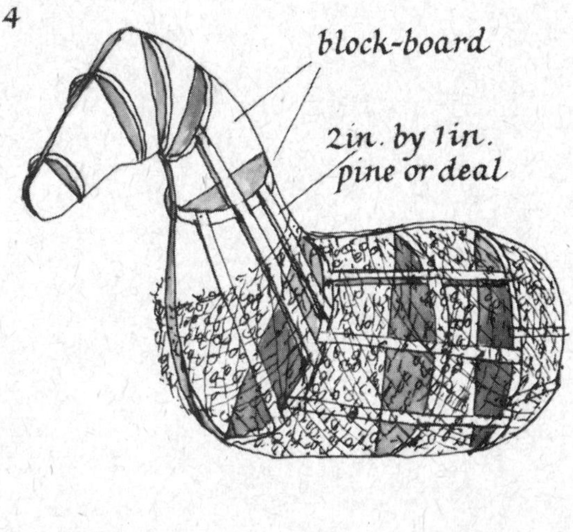

4. Examples of chicken-wire covering: this method can also be used on cane or wire frames

FIGURE 4

COVERING

Papier Mâché and Cloth

For a final covering for the framework papier mâché is most versatile. The principle on which it is based is that if many fragments of paper or cloth are soaked in glue and paste and then laid over each other, when they dry they fuse into a hard homogeneous skin. Papier mâché has a wide range of uses not only for covering but also for modelling, for obtaining varying textures, and for packing, shaping, decorating, and so on. It is perhaps the theatre's own special material, for in it are combined the cardinal qualities of strength and lightness.

The Preparation of Paper

As the cut edge of paper has only a little fibrous overhang *tear* it off and use only the centre of the sheet, for paper with torn edges mats much better in the papier mâché process. Tear the central portion of the sheet into irregular shapes about an inch square for small objects, three inches for medium ones and six for large, bearing in mind that the smaller the pieces the better the binding.

The Preparation of Cloth

For large areas and great strength canvas or cloth is best. Cut it into squares or strips *diagonally* across the grain for this will give you an easier lay when covering a curved surface. Sizes again, as with paper, vary according to the job. Generally, as already noted, cloth is used only for big objects, so your minimum size of a piece will be about five inches square and your maximum eighteen inches square.

A Note on Papers

Sugar paper and brown paper are good for making large-piece underlays. Newspaper is useful for general purposes and tissue and toilet papers are excellent finishers. If the papers are used in this order a smooth strong covering should result.

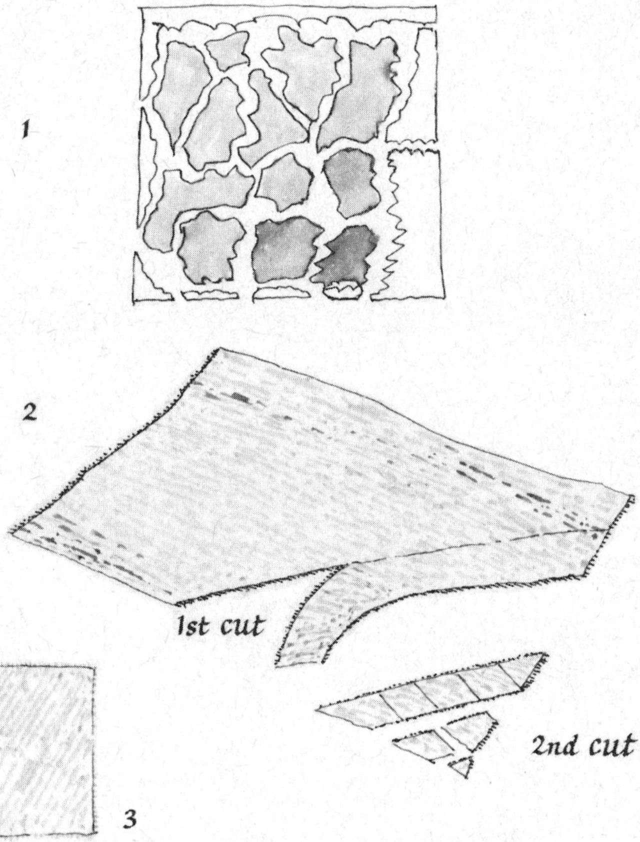

1. Sheet of prepared paper torn up using only the *inner* fragments
2. Cloth cut diagonally (on the cross) into strips, triangles, and rectangles
3. Detail: cloth with grain running diagonally gives better service

FIGURE 5

COVERING

Glue and Paste

These are the mediums that by soaking through and impregnating the fibrous material of paper and cloth, when dried and hardened, bind the layered fragments together into one whole.

To Prepare Paste

Take two buckets, fill one with water and let your torn paper lie in it to soak. Follow the directions on the bag of paste and prepare a mixture of a creamy thickness in your second bucket. Paste can be used only for paper.

To Prepare Glue

Carpenter's glue can be used for paper or cloth. It has the advantage over paste that it is stronger and has body. To make it, one needs a gas-ring, two buckets and water. Boil up a quarter to a third of a bucket of water and, putting the glue block or granules in the other bucket, place this in the boiling bucket. Stir the glue until it has melted into a piping hot fluid. It can be thinned with water, but its strength will diminish proportionately. Keep the glue as hot as the hand will stand, for the hotter the glue the greater its impregnation and binding power.

Size

This mild glue can also be used, but it lacks the strength of carpenter's glue and the cleanness of paste. Directions for making and using size are given on page 22. When used as a glue it is not left to cool.

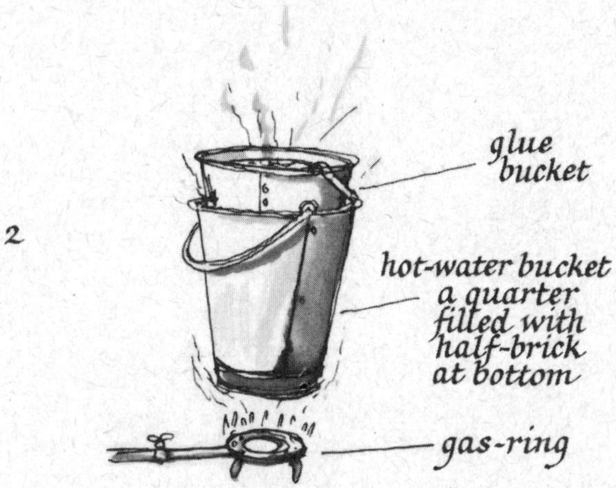

1. Paste machine 2. Glue machine

FIGURE 6

METHODS OF COVERING

Paper and Paste

Soak the paper in water and then dip it in the bucket of paste; crush and squeeze it until it is thoroughly impregnated with paste, wipe off the surplus and lay it over and round the object. Use the larger pieces first as a ground and cover this with smaller pieces. Overlay two or three times more and finish with tissue. Leave to dry in an airy place and, when thoroughly dry, paint with shellac. This will give a final bonding and a good surface for painting.

Paper and Glue

Dip unsoaked paper into hot glue, squeeze it gently to squeeze out the surplus glue and apply it in the same way as paste-treated paper. If you wish to build up a form, pulp the gluey paper in your hand and work it in with the flat-laid papier mâché. Glued paper will grow cold quickly, so work fast and precisely. After finishing off with tissue, leave to dry in a draughty place.

Canvas, Cloth, and Glue

Soak the canvas in hot glue and squeeze it out, lay it on, overlapping smoothly and crossing the pieces in an irregular manner. When covering a round shape wind the pieces in a spiral making the most of the give on the cross-grain of the material. When it is two or three layers thick, the tough hard skin will be a good base for finishing with paper. Leave to dry in an airy place.

Papier Mâché Modelling

Papier mâché which has been shredded and pulped in either glue or paste can be modelled quite easily. Nostrils, eyes, ears can be moulded with great delicacy provided that there is a key for them to lodge on.

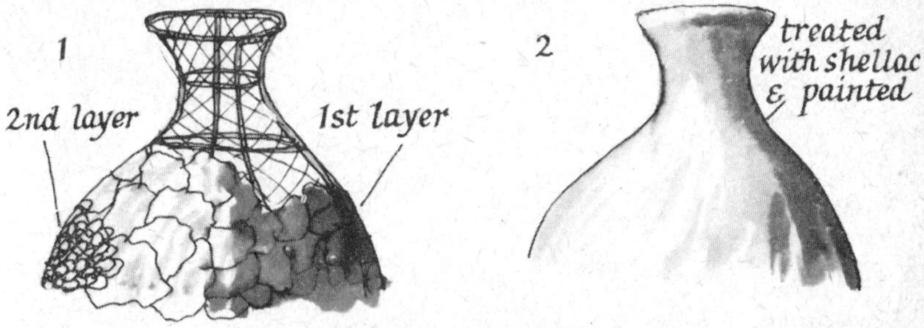

1. Frame covered with big then small pieces: repeat process three or four times, finishing with tissue
2. When thoroughly dried, treat with shellac and paint, finishing with glaze

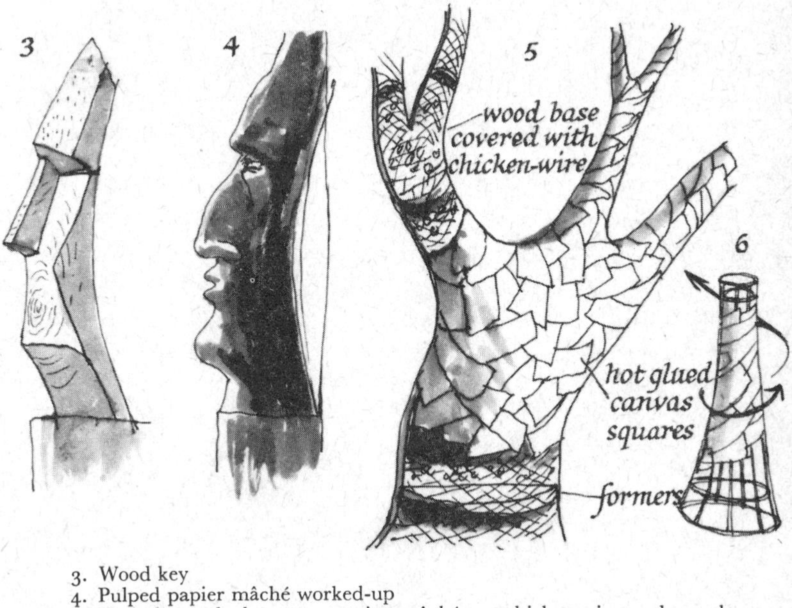

3. Wood key
4. Pulped papier mâché worked-up
5. Hot glue-soaked canvas papier mâché on chicken-wire and wood tree-frame
6. Spiralling cloth mâché on circular forms gives greater binding power and smoothness

FIGURE 7

PAINTING

PAINTING an object turns it from a dead shape into a living idea. By the intelligent use of colour, richness or dullness can be conveyed, a mood can be indicated, an object can be brought forward in importance on the stage or made to recede. By means of skilful painting, objects can be made to appear flatter or rounder, realistic or dreamlike, humorous or sombre.

Pigments

A pigment is the pure powder of a colour without the bonding medium. It can be bought in this state and mixed with the medium you prefer. The range of colours is infinite and the drawing opposite merely indicates the three primaries, with black and white. When choosing a pigment, remember that the finest ground is always the best.

Metallic Pigments

These are metallic filings of varying fineness and shades and can be used with very good effect on anything from jewellery to armour.

Mediums

Size

A bucket of boiling water into which a pound of size has been gently stirred is the most common and cheapest of the mediums. If however, the object painted is frequently handled it lacks sufficient durability and finish. To mix size with pigment pour it while still hot into the tin of colour that has previously been moistened and mix to the consistency and quantity that is needed. The lumps of pigment must be broken up with a brush, stick or the fingers until the mixture of size and pigment is quite smooth. Leave it to cool, then use.

Emulsion Medium and Glaze

These are water-plastic fluids and are mixed directly with the pigment. They can be watered down, but then lose lustre and strength in proportion. They have a better finish and binding

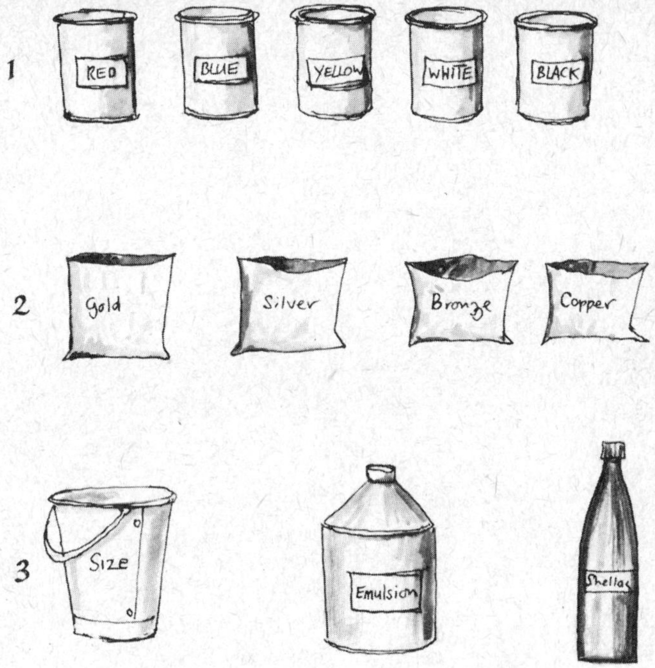

1. Three primary colours and black and white
2. Metallic pigments
3. Mediums

FIGURE 8

power than size, but are also more expensive. Glaze is a richer mixture than emulsion medium and very high glosses, such as would be needed on papier mâché pottery, can be obtained from it. These two mediums can also be used very satisfactorily in conjunction with metallic pigments.

Shellac (*French Polish*)

This medium, which makes an excellent finishing ground on papier mâché before painting is also used for the metallic pigments and for painting furniture.

PAINTING

Brushes

These are extremely important, for their fineness of quality will make or mar your painting performance as a blunt scalpel would a surgeon's. Good, well-kept brushes will give keener lines, smoother washes and more controlled textures. Too often property makers use cast-off scenic brushes. These are useless if there is to be a uniform quality throughout a stage setting. After using your brushes wash them thoroughly, for an overnight hardening will destroy the hair of the supplest brush.

Water-colour Brushes

Buy a selection of medium quality. These are useful for painting designs on pottery, features on faces, lettering, and a hundred and one jobs of detail.

Scenic Brushes

You will need one six-inch flat and one four-inch flat for laying-in, and a range of three-inch, two-inch, and one-inch flat and round brushes for general purposes.

Angled Fitches

These wedge-shaped brushes of a quarter of an inch, half-inch, one inch and one and a half inches are very useful for lining and big drawing.

Hog's-hair and Stencil Brushes

A few of these, large and small, are most helpful at times and it is worth having them in readiness.

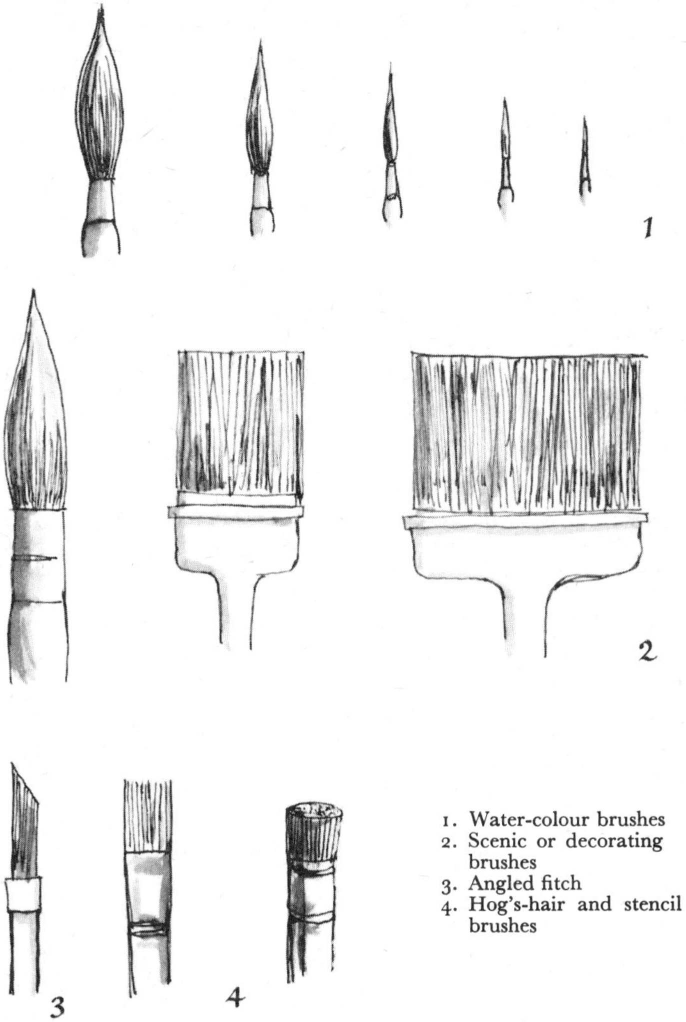

1. Water-colour brushes
2. Scenic or decorating brushes
3. Angled fitch
4. Hog's-hair and stencil brushes

FIGURE 9

PART II

PRACTICAL APPLICATIONS

In this section representative examples are illustrated in which the basic techniques of construction already described, as well as others, are utilized. It is hoped that by describing various processes in detail, it will be possible to give the reader a clear idea of the use and function of the materials used for making the actual props.

SIMPLE MASK

MODEL the face on a flat board from clay, wax or Plasticine. Cover it with petroleum jelly to act as an anti-stick barrier, and then lay two layers of water-soaked but unpasted papier mâché as a second safeguard against the mask's sticking to the clay master. For the next four layers use paste-soaked papier mâché and bandage and after working-up the features finish with tissue. When thoroughly dry, carefully prise it off the clay master, clean and papier-mâché the inside to reinforce it, and leave to dry again. Paint with shellac when ready, to give the final binding, and paint the surface. After painting, glue on hair, moustaches and beards of string, wool, hemp, or rough felt as required. Cut out the eye spaces and fix elastic tape on each temple, adjusting the length of the tape. The mask is now complete.

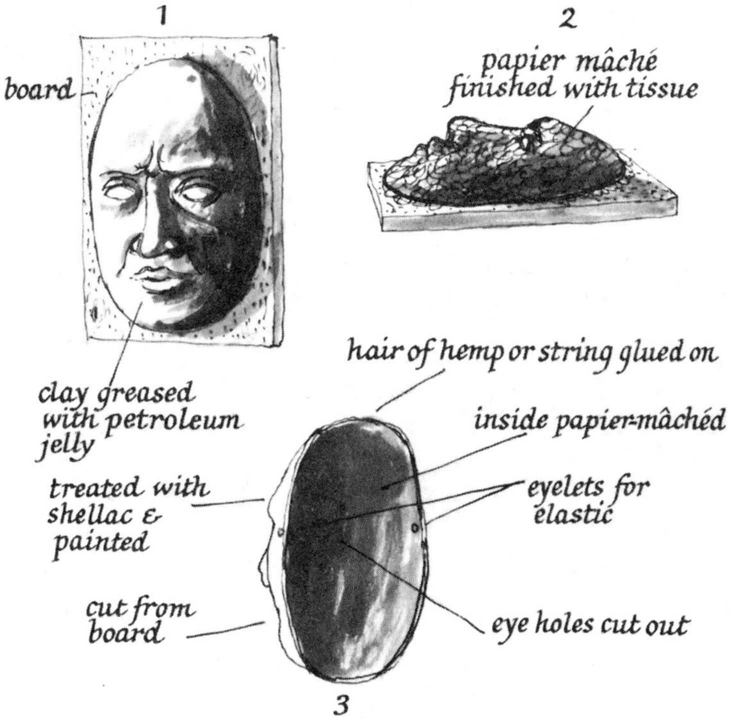

1. Clay master modelled on baseboard
2. Clay master covered with papier mâché and left to dry
3. Mask detached from baseboard and ready for hair, eyes, and elastic tape

FIGURE 10

WIRED MASKS

THE wired mask is stronger and more durable than the simple mask; a further advantage is that the shape can be more controlled and elaborated. To construct it, make a galvanized-wire frame and cover it with papier mâché inside and outside, work-up the features and leave to dry. When it is dry coat with shellac to harden and give a good surface for painting. Paint and decorate with wool, string, hemp, raffia felt, and with sequins for eyes. Where the eyes of the mask do not correspond with the actor's, cut holes to match his and overlay them with gauze painted the same colour as the mask. This enables the actor to see without the audience suspecting that he is looking through the cheeks. Pad the inside of the mask with felt, cloth or sponge rubber. Those illustrated opposite are just face masks, but there is no reason why a mask to cover the whole head should not be made if required, provided that enough space is left for the actor's head to pass through at the neck.

1. Ugly sister
2. King
3. Cinderella
4. African tribal mask
5 and 6. Japanese mask and its construction
7. Greek tragedian
8 and 9. Greek mask and its construction

FIGURE 11

PORTRAIT BUST

SOMETIMES it is necessary to have an actual portrait bust of one of the characters, for example, of Julius Caesar. To achieve this, a clay master portrait of the actor playing the part must first be modelled from life. This is done by the usual process of setting up an armature and packing clay round it; the rest depends on the modeller's talents.

When the clay head is finished, cover it with papier mâché, beginning with three layers of unpasted paper, followed by as many layers of paste-soaked sugar paper as will still retain the subtlety and crispness of the underlying clay master. When it is thoroughly dry, cut with a sharp knife as shown in the drawing, and clean out the inside and treat it with shellac. Fix the two halves together over a wire or wooden skeleton, packing it with newspaper. Papier-mâché the joins so that they are absolutely secure and when they are dry shellac the whole two or three times. It is now ready to be painted either with bronze metallic pigment, with green and black staining or with stone colours. If it is well made the bust will look quite authentic and will have the advantage of being light.

To model carved drapery, dip canvas, scrim, or gauze into hot glue or a bowl of wet plaster of Paris, drape as it is wanted and leave. When dry, paint.

To make plaster, pour small quantities of the powder gradually into a bowl of water; when it becomes creamy it begins to thicken, and will then take only a minute or two to harden completely.

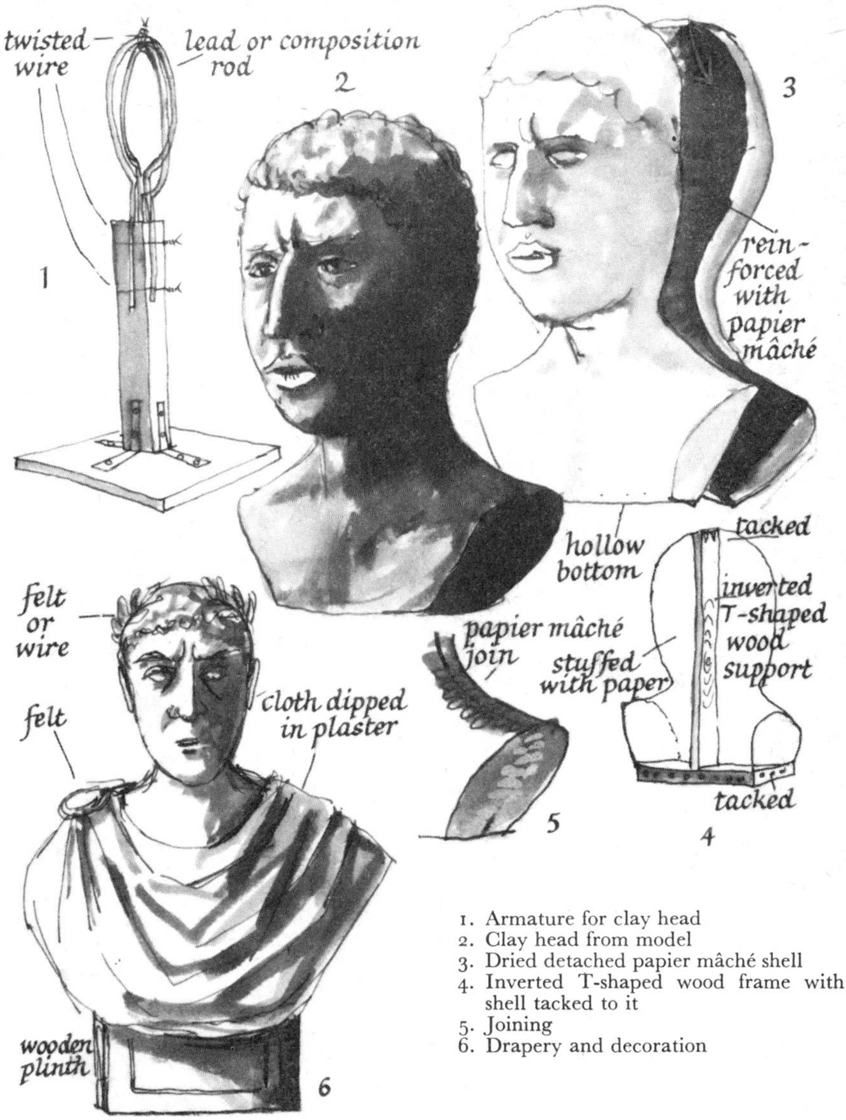

1. Armature for clay head
2. Clay head from model
3. Dried detached papier mâché shell
4. Inverted T-shaped wood frame with shell tacked to it
5. Joining
6. Drapery and decoration

FIGURE 12

SHIPS' FIGURE-HEADS

CONSTRUCT a framework of galvanized wire, cover the large areas with chicken-wire and papier mâché made from canvas or paper, and finished with tissue. Model the folds and features with pulped papier mâché and when dry, fix with glue or sew on with thin wire the details, made from thin smooth felt, which when soaked with shellac stiffens. Work the hair with cord, string, wool or raffia. When it is finished paint and add the buttons, braids, and sequins.

1. William Penn
2. Medusa
3. Head and snake construction of Medusa

4. Construction of Red Indian
5. Susquehanna

FIGURE 13

A THRONE

CONSTRUCT the basic chair from timber. Add the wire figures and from felt cut decorative shapes and embossings. Papier-mâché the wire figures and marry them with the tacked felt elaborations into one solid mass. When dry, treat the felt and the papier mâché with shellac to stiffen them, and work-up with paint, jewellery, glitter, etc. into the appearance of carved wood or worked metal.

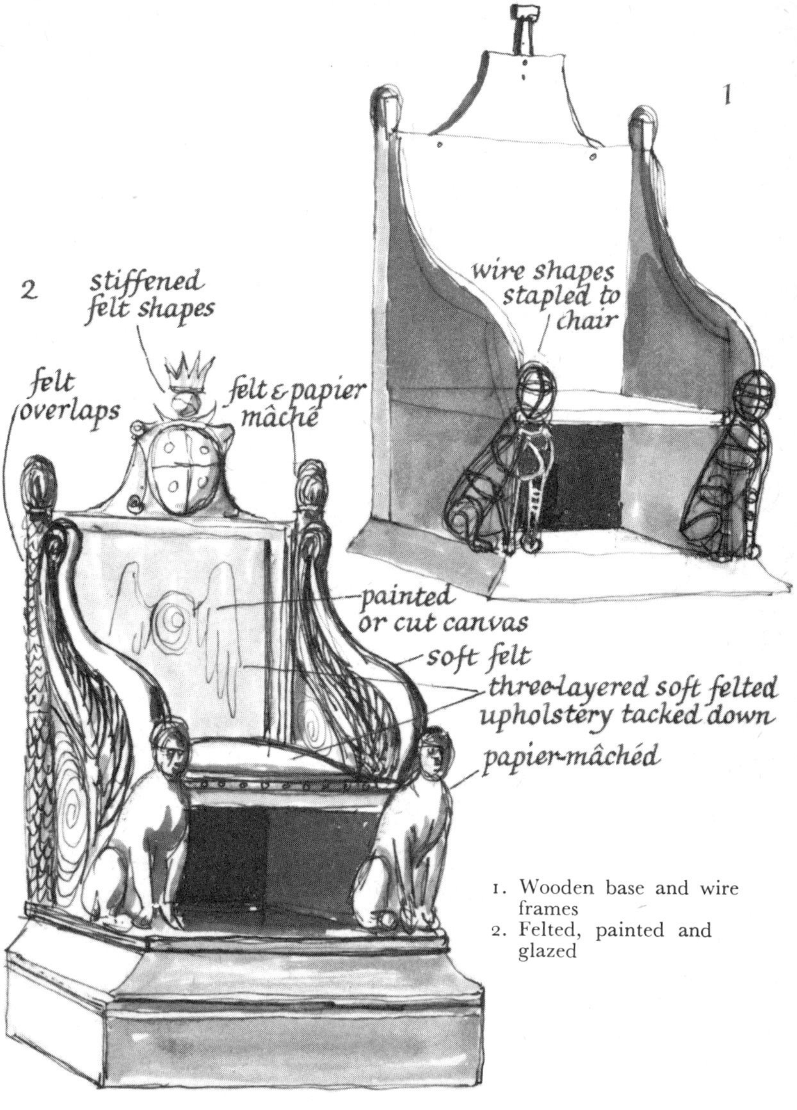

1. Wooden base and wire frames
2. Felted, painted and glazed

FIGURE 14

CROWNS

Construct a framework of galvanized wire and cover it with papier mâché. When it is dry, paint it with metallic paint using reds, browns, and blacks to give the appearance of mellowness. Jewellery and decoration can be made of cotton-wool, felt, rope or cord set with sequins, beads, bottle-tops, sweet-papers, wine gums, stones, coins, buttons, braids, silver and gold twisted wires, and, of course, cheap jewels. If very large jewels are needed these can be made from pulped papier mâché or cotton-wool soaked in paste, shaped and moulded and painted with metallic paints and glitter or covered with transparent screwed-up sweet-paper.

This open crown is the basis of all crowns and more elaborate ones can be made simply by adding arches of wire, velvet caps, and more jewellery.

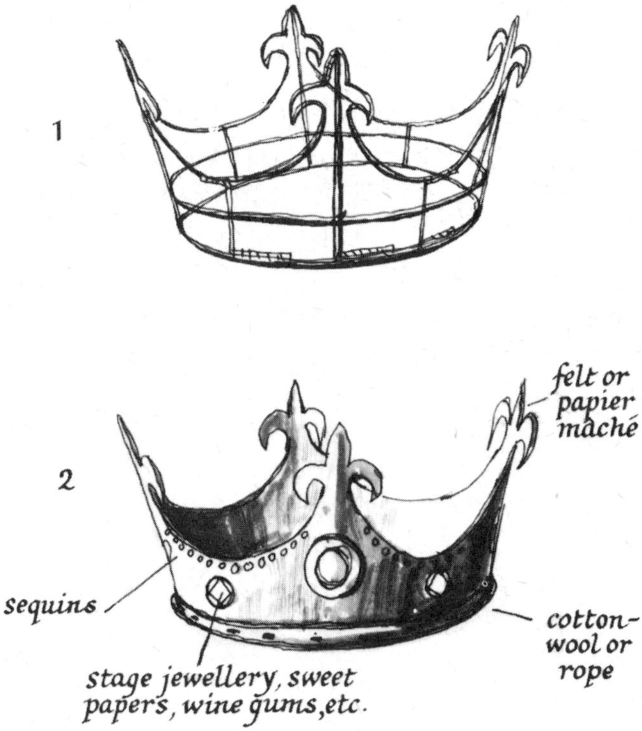

1. Wire frame
2. Painting and decoration

FIGURE 15

CROWN JEWELS, CROZIER, AND ORB

THE sceptre is made of a two-foot length of one-and-a-half-inch pole drilled at the top down four inches. Two or three double or looped wires are pushed down the hole and are secured by driving a screw into the pole, passing it through the loops. Additional wires are taped in, and from these the eagle's wings and body frame are formed. Cover it with hot glue and pulped papier mâché, and work to the final shape. The other decorations are made of felt which is tacked to the pole and papier-mâchéd. When it is all dry, paint with metallic paint, add jewellery as in crown-making.

The crozier is made in the same way as the sceptre, except that the wires are shaped into a curling hook. The lamb can be made of shellac-stiffened felt stuck to the taped wire. The decorations on the hook and handle are made of felt tacked to the pole and covered with papier mâché. Paint it with metallic paints of both silver and gold.

The orb can be made from a large wooden ball drilled with holes into which wires are set and wedged, or it can be constructed from a wire sphere stuffed with paper. Felt, metallic paint, and mock jewellery will complete the object.

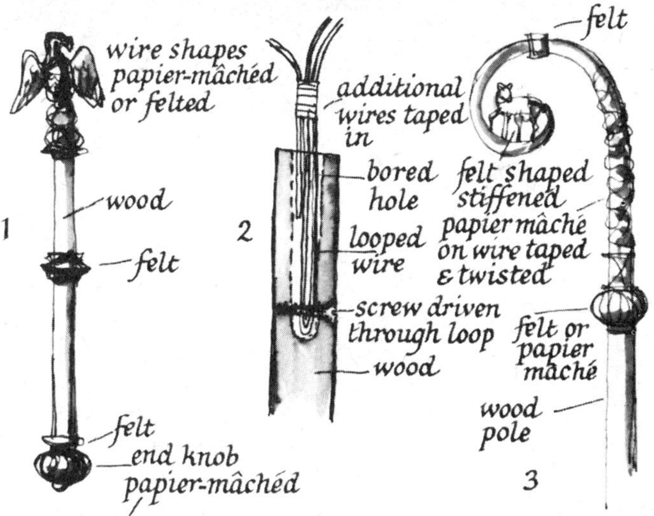

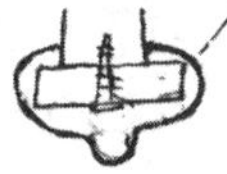

1. Sceptre and baton
2. Method of securing wire ends in hole by screwing through wire loop
3. Crozier

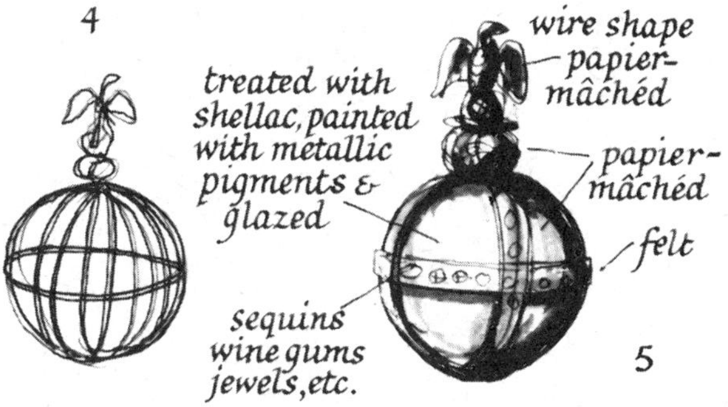

4. Wire frame or orb
5. Decorated orb

FIGURE 16

JEWELLERY

THE necklace is made of smooth felt glued or tacked upon a wood base. The fleur-de-lis and other raised decorations are also made of felt, cut to shape and stiffened with two or three coats of shellac and the felt shapes sewn on to the thin chain attached to the wooden block are treated in the same way. The jewels themselves are made of anything, glass, sequins, bottle-tops, wine gums, sweet-paper wrappings, glitter, silver and gold foils and wires, coins, pearls, stones, braids, and cheap jewellery. Large jewels can be made from papier mâché or paste-soaked cotton-wool covered with transparent sweet-paper. The felt is painted with metallic pigments.

The medallion is simply a chain attached to a shape of wood, built-up with felt or papier mâché. Heads, patterns, and symbols can be made to look convincingly metallic by skilful painting.

Rings are made by twisting silver and gold wires into a loop and making a large jewelled decoration at the knot. To make a band-ring careful taping with either cloth or paper masking-tape is needed.

Bracelets and bands are made of felt sewn or glued to taped wire stiffened with shellac, painted and jewelled.

A jewel box or chest can be a ready-made box covered with felt, studs, metallic foils and painted, with the lid constructed of curved skin-ply on shaped formers.

1. Ring of taped and twisted wire
2. Necklace
3. Medallion
4. Bracelet
5. Jewel-box

FIGURE 17

A CANDLESTICK

UPON a heavy wooden base build the under-form of twisted and taped galvanized wire, with at the top a wooden or metallic tube and a fixture to hold the flame-shaped bulb. Draw the flex through the tube and tape it down the body of the candle to pierce and pass out of the bottom of the stand to the switch and power-socket. Papier-mâché the candle, burying the flex and working-up the design with pulped papier mâché and felt. Model a few drops of grease on the candle itself with glue and paint the candlestick with metallic pigment.

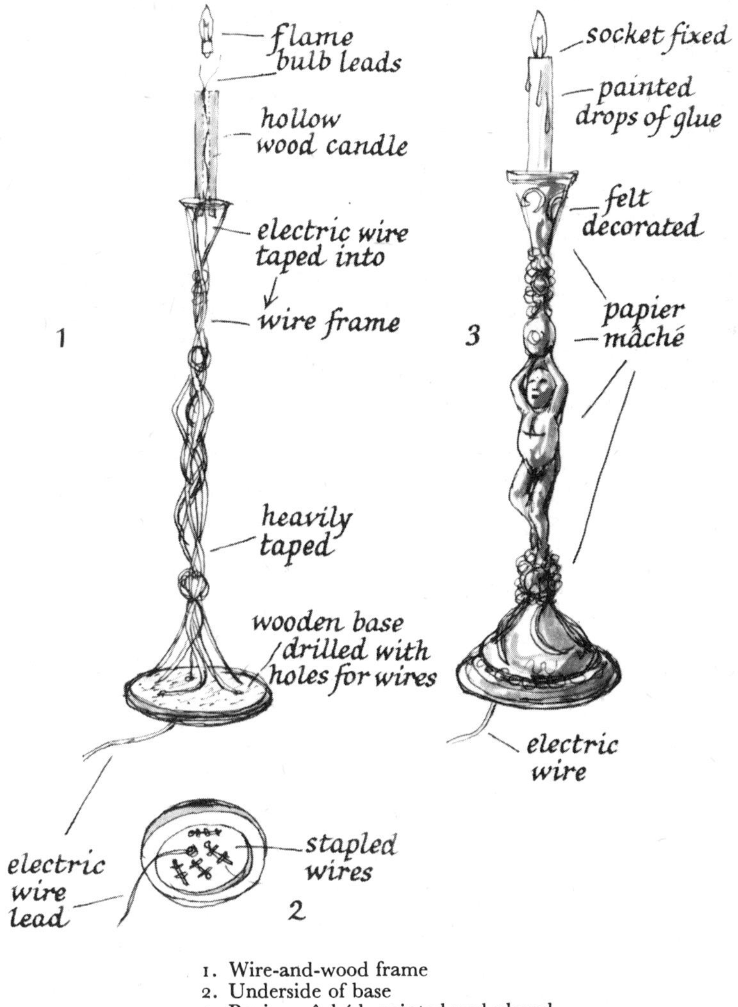

1. Wire-and-wood frame
2. Underside of base
3. Papier-mâchéd, painted and glazed

FIGURE 18

LAMPS, CHANDELIERS, AND FIRES

An oil-lamp of almost any shape can be made of galvanized wire with the battery, switch, bulb-holder, and wiring system taped in and covered with papier mâché. The stud switch can be worked in easily with the decoration and the bulb will of course be flame-shaped.

Chandeliers can be constructed of fretted and profiled block-board fixed to a strong central hub or worked cane locked by wire. Both lamps and chandeliers are decorated with taped galvanized wire and glued and shellac-stiffened felt. The candles can be made of metal or wooden tubing with flame-shaped bulbs set in holders. The wiring system is taped to the bare frame before being buried under the papier mâché and felt finish.

Lamp-posts are made of taped galvanized wire, wood, or strap-iron with decoration of shellac-stiffened felt. The wiring can be dealt with by any amateur electrician.

Stage fires are made of a lamp, and crumpled and dyed gauze or canvas. Coals, wood, logs can be real or can be painted or papier mâché shapes with the light glinting through. Beware of overheating; leave vents for the hot air to escape.

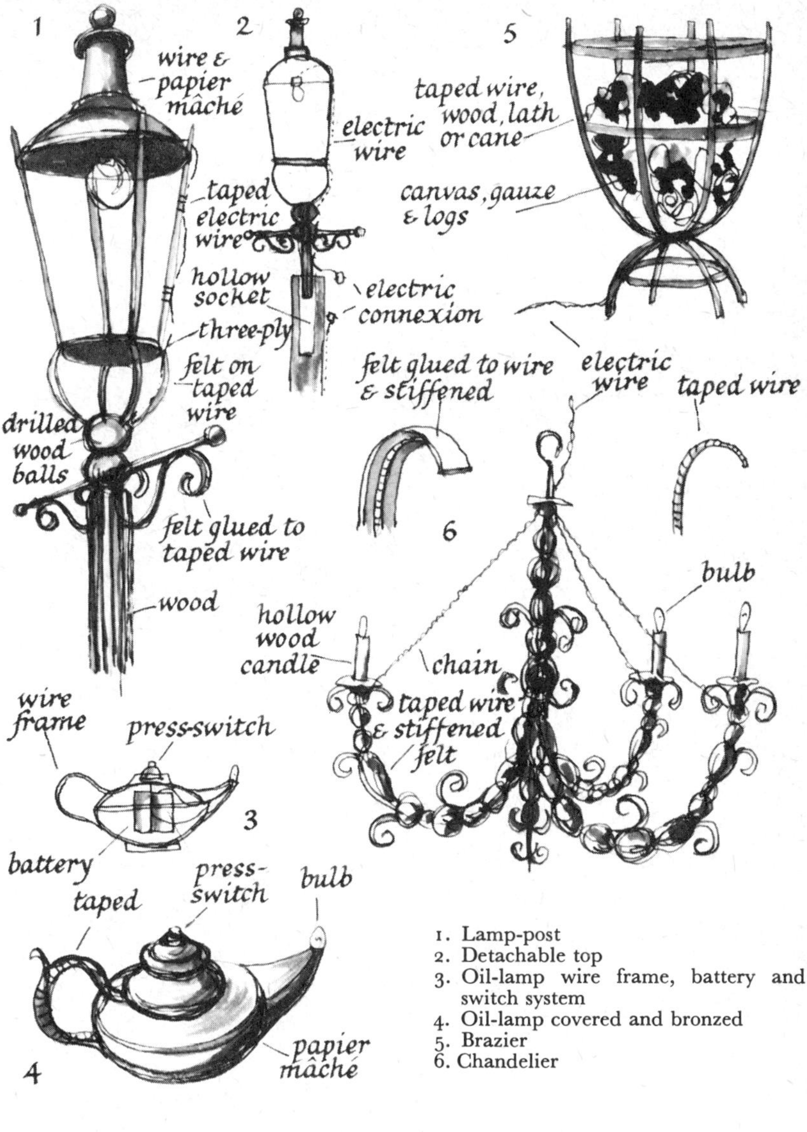

1. Lamp-post
2. Detachable top
3. Oil-lamp wire frame, battery and switch system
4. Oil-lamp covered and bronzed
5. Brazier
6. Chandelier

Figure 19

ARCHITECTURAL DETAIL

Columns, arches, mouldings, etc., after having been constructed of timber formers, galvanized wire, and chicken-wire are covered with canvas (*see* page 20) and worked-up with paper and pulped papier mâché. Some decorations can be dealt with more effectively by gluing felt to taped wire and stiffening it with shellac.

If you are constructing a tympanum make the wired figures separately before taping them into the structure. When this method of prefabricating is adopted the job can be finished quickly, while at the same time delicacy of structure is achieved.

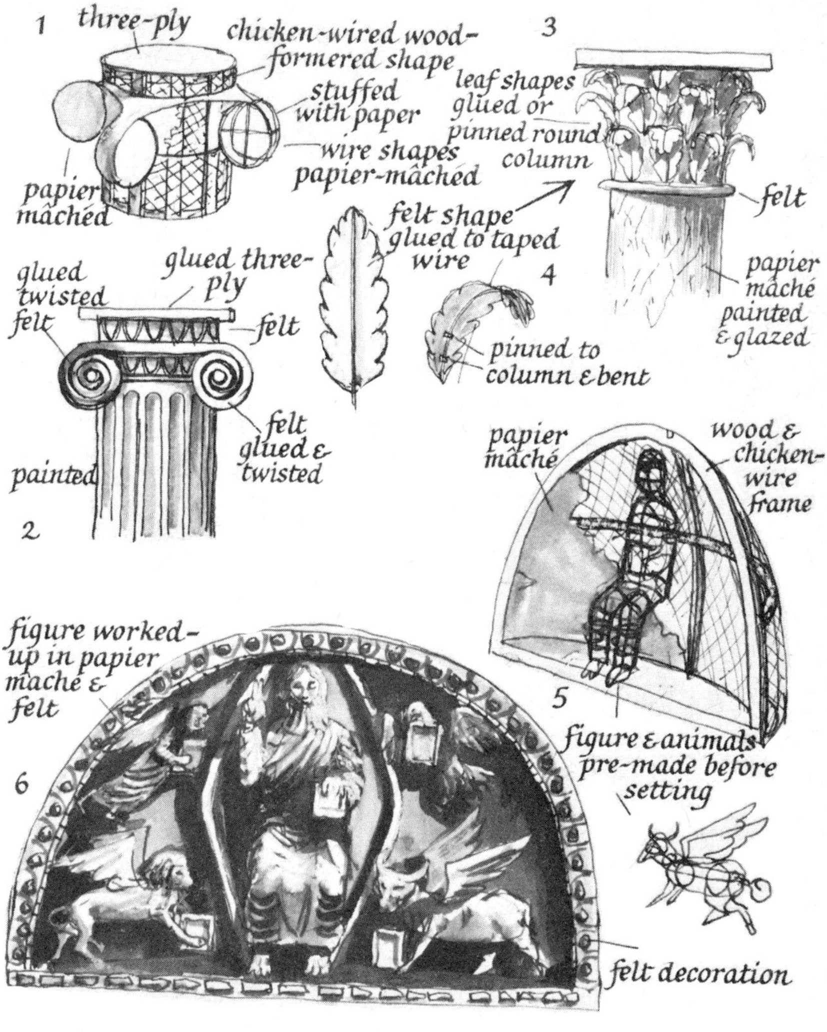

1. Framework for column head
2 and 3. Finished jobs
4. Felt leaves and their attachment
5. Frame with first figure of wire set in
6. Worked-up figures of felt and papier mâché

FIGURE 20

WOOD OR STONE MONUMENTAL PLAQUE

Build up out of taped wire a frame of the larger shapes and staple these down on to a base-board edged with beading. Individual units, e.g. a cornucopia, may be made separately and stapled on afterwards. After covering the plaque with papier mâché and letting it dry, develop the detail with pinned and glued felt, card, cord, masking tape and stiff parcel-ribbon, working-up the sharpness and delicacy of the objects. When they are complete and dry, paint the whole plaque with three or four coats of shellac to bind and harden before finally painting them to look like wood or stone.

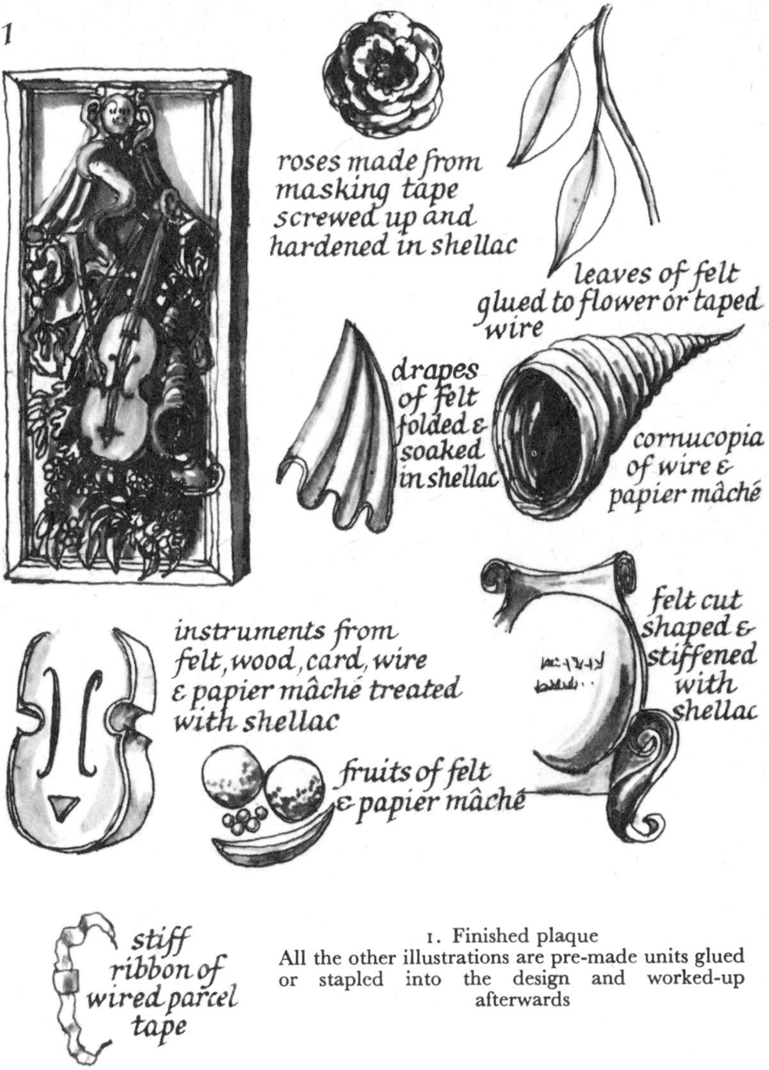

1. Finished plaque
All the other illustrations are pre-made units glued or stapled into the design and worked-up afterwards

Figure 21

IDOLS, MUMMIES, AND SCULPTURE

STAGE sculpture must look heavy and yet be light. This result is achieved by building up the basic shape with wire, cane or wooden formers and covering it with chicken-wire. After papier-mâchéing it with canvas and overlaying with paper, work-up the detail with felt and pulped papier mâché. Skilful painting will give it the appearance of granite or metal as required.

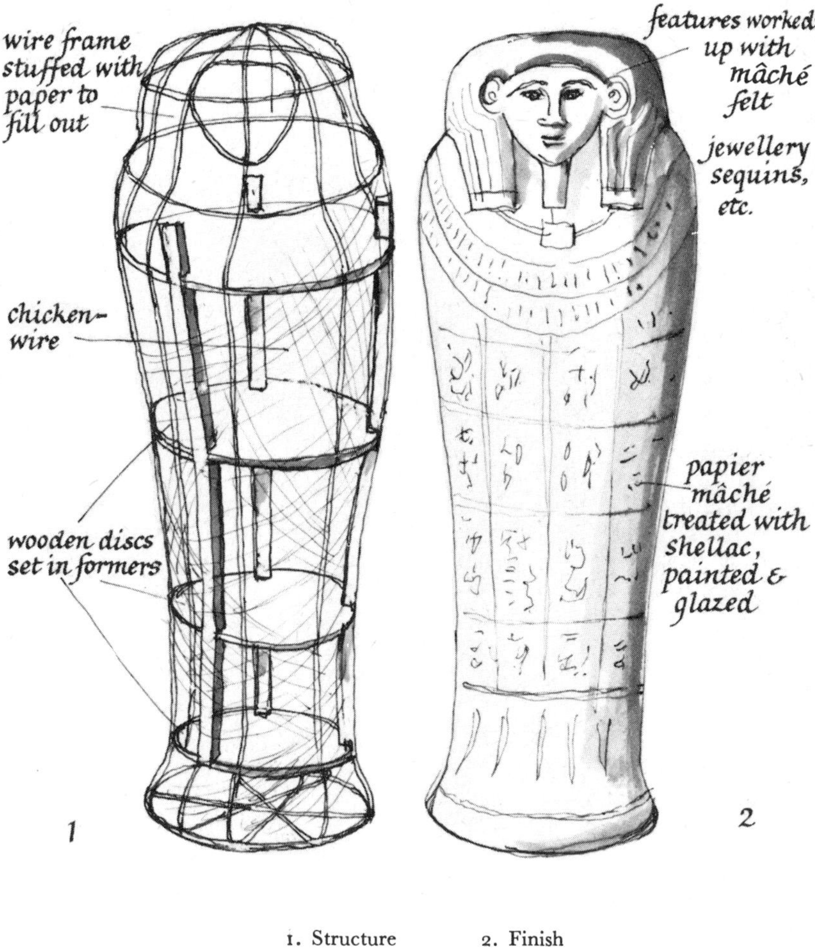

1. Structure 2. Finish

Figure 22

FRAMES

To make a decorated mirror frame, cut a shape out of three-ply and cover it with a sheet of silver foil paper, carefully smoothing with a rag and paste. Study your reference book for frame-carving of the period and cut out felt shapes in the same character. Tack these along the edge, just overlapping the silver foil, curling and curving them about and into one another as in the carving. When you have built up a pattern, shellac once and begin to mould and work the felt into its final shape. After each succeeding application of shellac the felt will become progressively harder and eventually after about five coats, it should be quite stiff when dry. Beware of staining the silver foil as you apply the shellac and when you gild or paint.

The picture frame is made in exactly the same way as the mirror frame. To make a false canvas use the rough side of hardboard sized twice: this will give a good surface on which to paint your picture.

SKULL

Construct a framework of galvanized wire, stuff it with paper to fill out, and cover with papier mâché. The features can be worked finely in pulped papier mâché. The teeth are made of wood and embedded in the papier mâché. When it is dry sand paper it and treat with shellac two or three times, allow to harden, and paint it, finishing with a glaze.

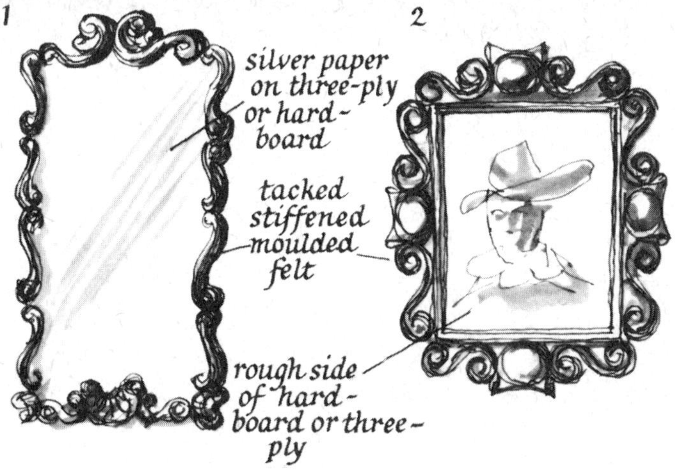

1. Mirror frame 2. Picture frame

FIGURE 23

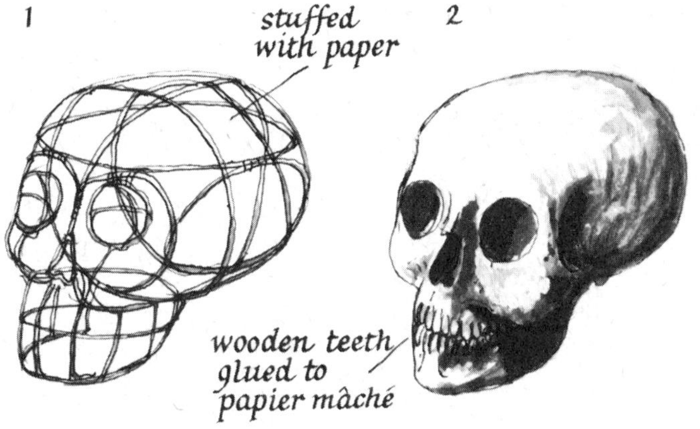

1. Structure 2. Finish

FIGURE 24

CELESTIAL BODIES

To make these medieval symbols, all that is needed is a three-ply base to which taped wires are stapled or fuse-wire sewn. On to these taped-wire arms, braids, sequins, metallic foils, and glitters may be glued. Faceted stars that will catch and reflect light extremely effectively on the stage can be made from metallic foils by anyone skilful in cutting, scoring, bending and moulding. This skill is needed for the sun shown opposite, which can be drawn, by means of hooks in the back of the base-board, across the stage on fishing-lines; so can the moon and comet. Glitter may be sprinkled on to paste on back-drop gauzes to give the effect of distant twinkling stars, the shapes of nearer ones are drawn in paste and sprinkled with glitter, which is supplied in fine to coarse ranges of particles, according to the kind of texture you want.

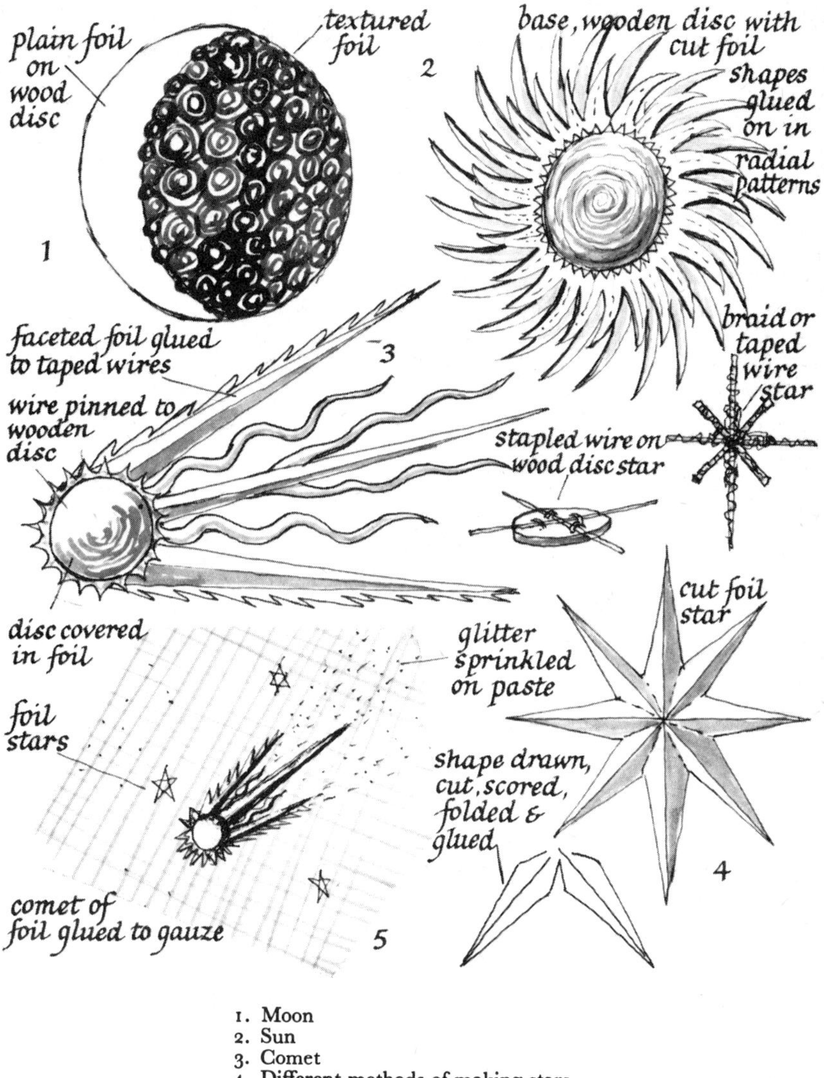

1. Moon
2. Sun
3. Comet
4. Different methods of making stars
5. Comet and stars on gauze back-drop

FIGURE 25

IMPERIAL EAGLE

A WOODEN shape is cut out from three-ply and carved blocks are screwed or glued to its chest, wings, feet, and head. Felt shapes, as indicated in the drawing, are cut and tacked down in overlapping sequences. Papier mâché is applied to work-up the head and the wire of the feet, and the whole object is finished off with five coats of shellac to stiffen and mould the felt feathers. Paint to represent wood or metal.

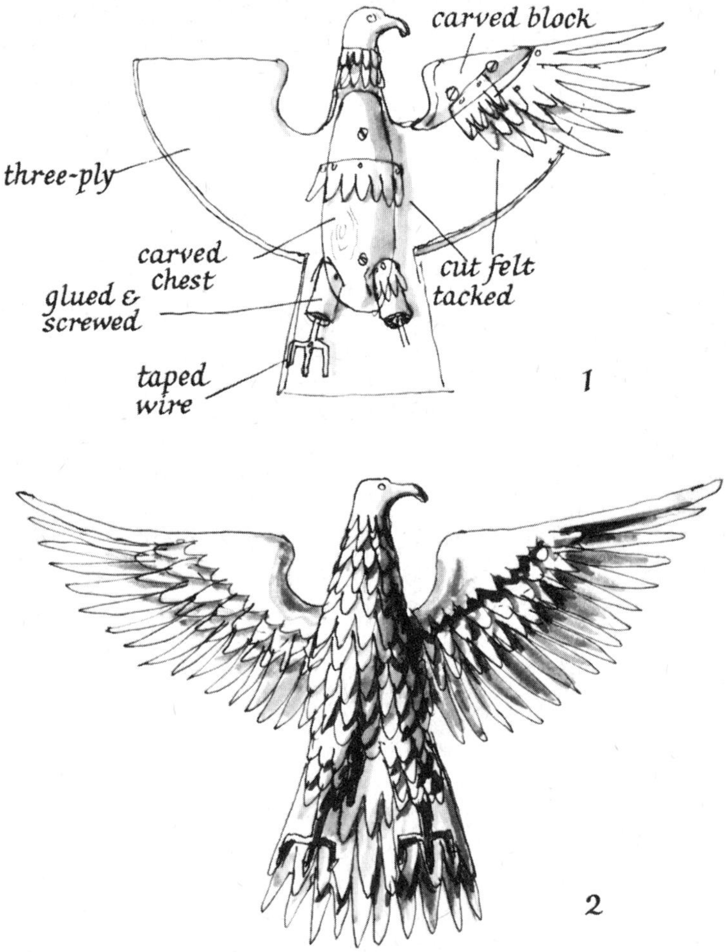

1. Base-board 2. Treated with shellac and painted

FIGURE 26

ANIMAL HEADS

Build the basic shape out of galvanized wire, stuff it with paper and cover with papier mâché. Paint the skin with glue and while it is still wet brush it over with loose felt, leaving deposits of hair and texture behind. On very hairy places stick felt or animal baize. For manes and beards use rope, hemp, string, wool, raffia, shredded felt, or shredded cloth. Spray with methylated spirit dye or paint with a dryish brush to avoid smoothing the texture away. For eyes use beads or sequins.

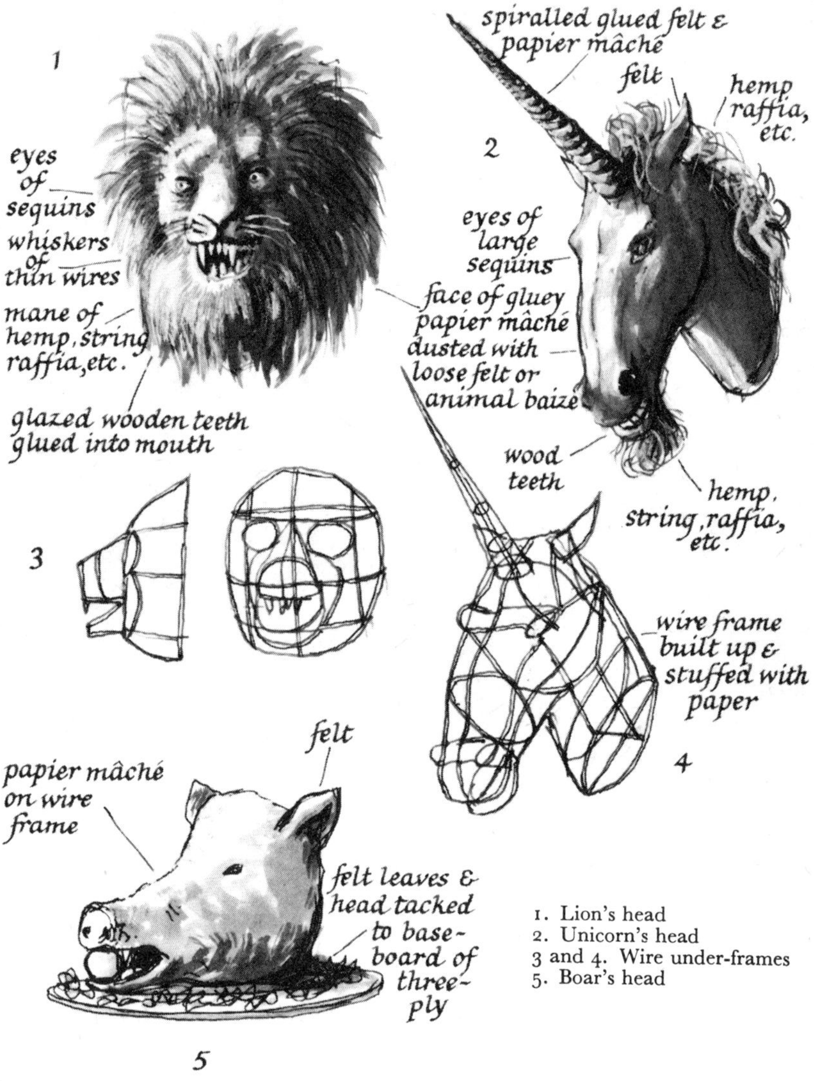

1. Lion's head
2. Unicorn's head
3 and 4. Wire under-frames
5. Boar's head

FIGURE 27

VULTURE

Construct the body unit and wings out of galvanized wire, stuff it with paper and cover with papier mâché. Use real feathers or felt cut-out shapes, gluing them in overlapping bands from the tail towards the head. Cover the quill ends of the feathers with gauze and smooth out over the leading edge of the wings. Methylated spirit dye can be used to stain the feathers and felt (after they have been stiffened with shellac). Paint the head sallow pink and use black beads or sequins for the eyes. Bind the wire of the feet with tape and soak with clogging glue.

To obtain a slow sinister flapping motion when it is drawn across the stage, construct the mechanism shown in tough steel wire.

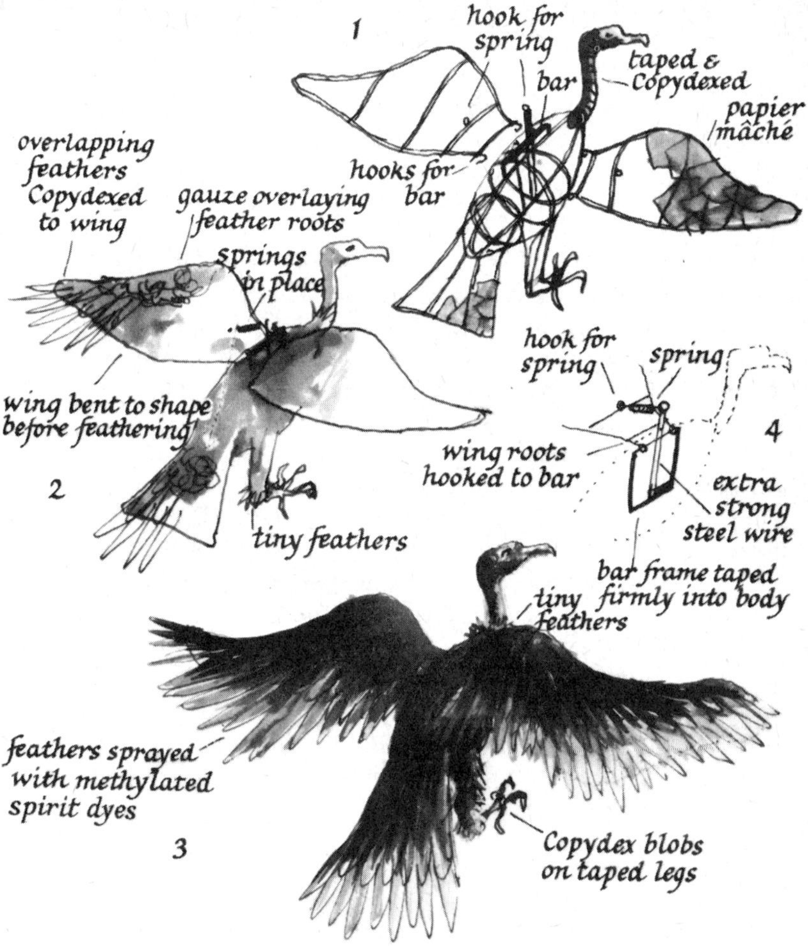

1. Framework and papier mâché covering
2. Applying feathers and gauze
3. Finished bird
4. Wing-flapping mechanism

FIGURE 28

SIMPLE PUPPET

HERE is a formula that can be used for making any character, with the necessary variation of face and clothes.

The face is a carved unit of wood with a hole bored at the base for the hollow tube of wood of the neck to be set in. The tube has a long wire loop passing through it at each end. At the upper end the loop is hooked into a screw set in the roof of the head drilling. The neck tube should be fairly loose to give a good head movement. The face is of papier mâché or plastic wood moulded and painted. The hair is of string or hemp glued to the scalp. The chest and pelvis are of cut and carved hardwood (mahogany or teak), with screw-eyes connecting in interlinked couplings with the arms and neck.

The legs of hardwood are joined to the pelvis by a tough bent-wire pivot giving a forward and backward movement only. The knee joint is neatly cut and carved and drilled and a pin or wire fitted as a pivot. Note the locking device in the carving of the joint so that the legs do not bend forwards unnaturally. The feet are also jointed in this manner and toes of felt, or shoes, can easily be added.

The arms of hardwood are jointed as the legs but are connected by large screw-eyes to the shoulders. The hands are likewise joined with screw-eyes and the fingers are of felt or taped or papier-mâchéd wire. All the limbs have plates of lead screwed along them to give a weight for the controller to work against and to give the maximum tension so necessary to make the puppet work well.

The tiny screw-eyes, for strings, thick thread, or fishing line, are fixed on either side of the head, shoulders, wrists and knees, and one in the small of the back. The strings rise up to the controller, a large grip of wood with a fixed bar for the head and a loose detachable bar for the legs. Between theses bars are two independently moving tough-wire armatures for separate arm motions and a pivoted unit of wire and bar for the shoulders and the small of the back.

To work, hold the grip in the left hand, using the fingers to manipulate the arms, shoulders and back. Tilting the grip from side to side will move the head, and up-ending will affect the back and shoulders. The right hand holds the detached bar for the legs and should be held forward of the puppet as it is led. When the line lengths have been adjusted, practice will reveal manipulation techniques.

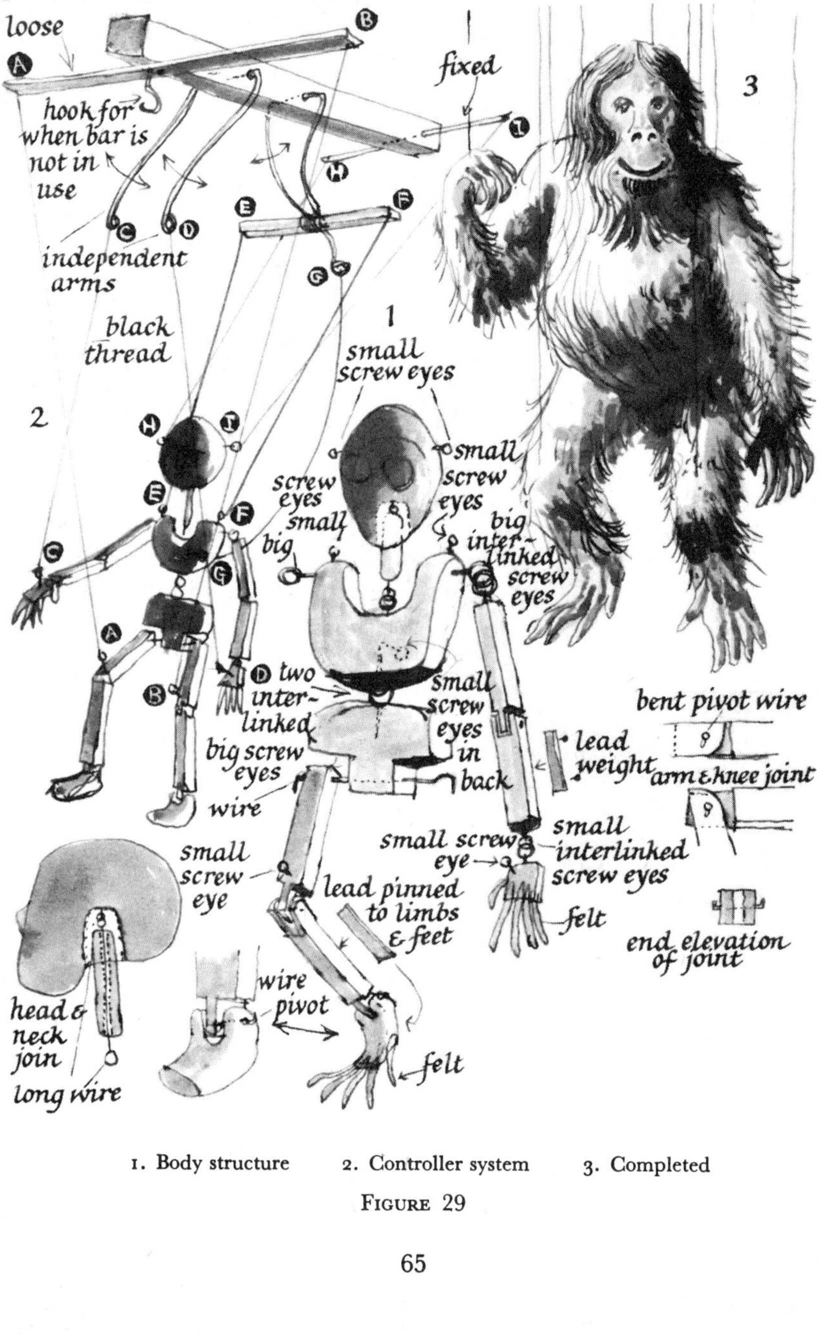

1. Body structure 2. Controller system 3. Completed

Figure 29

TIGER AND CROCODILE

To make a tiger-skin, construct the head out of galvanized wire and fix it to the flat body shape cut from felt by gluing or sewing with wire. Cover the head with papier mâché, marrying the neck to the skin, and while it is still wet from glue, dust the head and neck with loose felt to leave a fur texture. For more hairy parts glue on felt or animal baize. Paint the stripes with a dryish brush and round the edges glue under the skin a black border, projecting about an inch out. To finish, glue in beads or sequins for the eyes.

To construct a magician's crocodile or alligator build the shape from galvanized wire and cover with chicken-wire and papier mâché. Glue on felt ridges and drop dollops of glue all over the body to give the appearance of a gnarled skin. Paint with shellac and pigments to work up horniness and stick in sequins for the eyes.

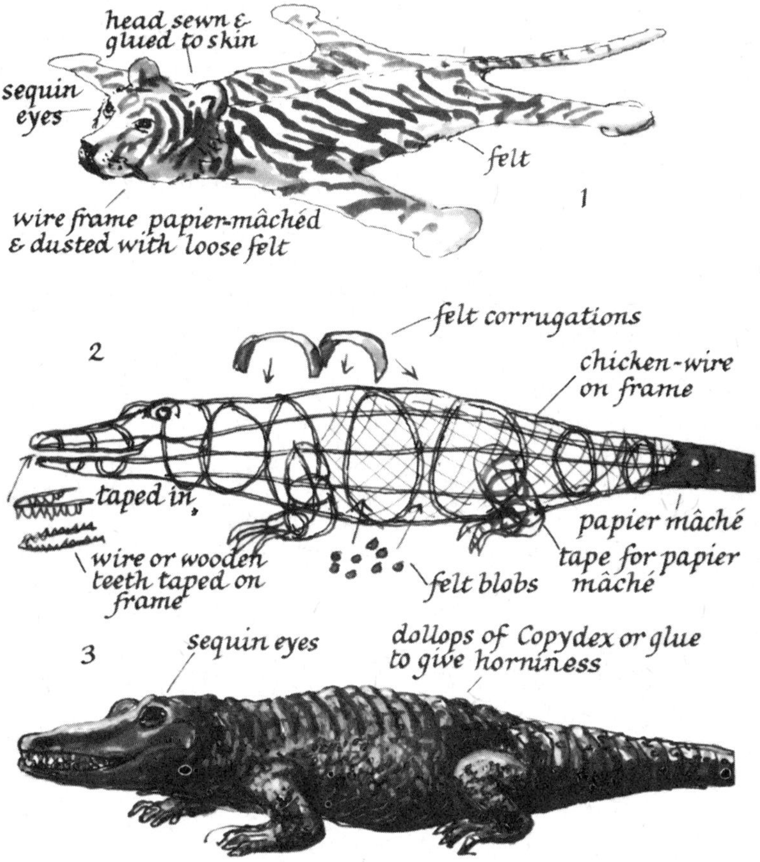

1. Tiger skin 2. Frame for crocodile 3. Finished job

FIGURE 30

FISH

THE first method of making a fish (shown opposite) is to cut the shape out of two pieces of cloth, sew them together, turn inside out and fill with rags, paper, or sawdust. After sewing on fins of stiffened cloth, paint with a high glaze or cover with polythene and finish off with sequin eyes.

The second method is to take an inch-square piece of wood of a length depending on the particular fish and to pin to it the shapes of the tail and fins cut from Cinemoid, allowing for the thickness of the body. Then, taping newspaper round and round to fill out the shape, cover the whole with papier mâché, marrying the fins and tail into the flow of the line. Paint the body and fins appropriately, using french enamel varnish on the Cinemoid. Glue in sequins for the eyes and glaze heavily or cover with polythene.

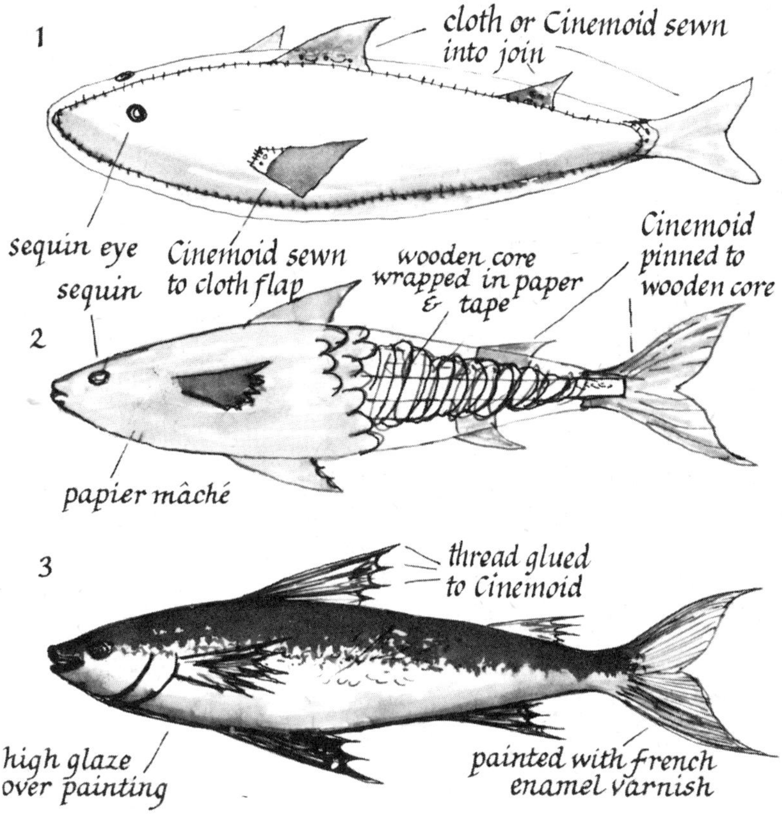

1. First method using sewn, stuffed cloth
2. Second method using wood and papier mâché
3. Painted and decorated

Figure 31

PROCESSIONAL DRAGON

THIS large but light monster is constructed of a wire frame taped to cane hoops which are secured firmly to three two-inch hand-poles by which it is held. Build three units of wire, one for the head, one for the body, including the legs and wings, and one for the curling tail. When these are firm and rigid, tape the units together, simultaneously binding them on the heat-bent cane hoops.

This should form a light but strong skeleton that for further working can be tacked temporarily in an upright position to the side of a long table.

The covering is of Jap silk. This is secured by gluing or sewing along the skeleton, which has been taped throughout to give a surface for gluing. The head, body, wings, legs, and tail are covered with different coloured tailored sections. Additional decoration is made by gluing and sewing on lappets, streamers, and other fluttering details that look very striking as the dragon is carried at speed.

The painting is done with Tapestry Medium, as this does not spread too much on Jap silk. Sequins, glitter, and metallic foils also add to the scintillating effect.

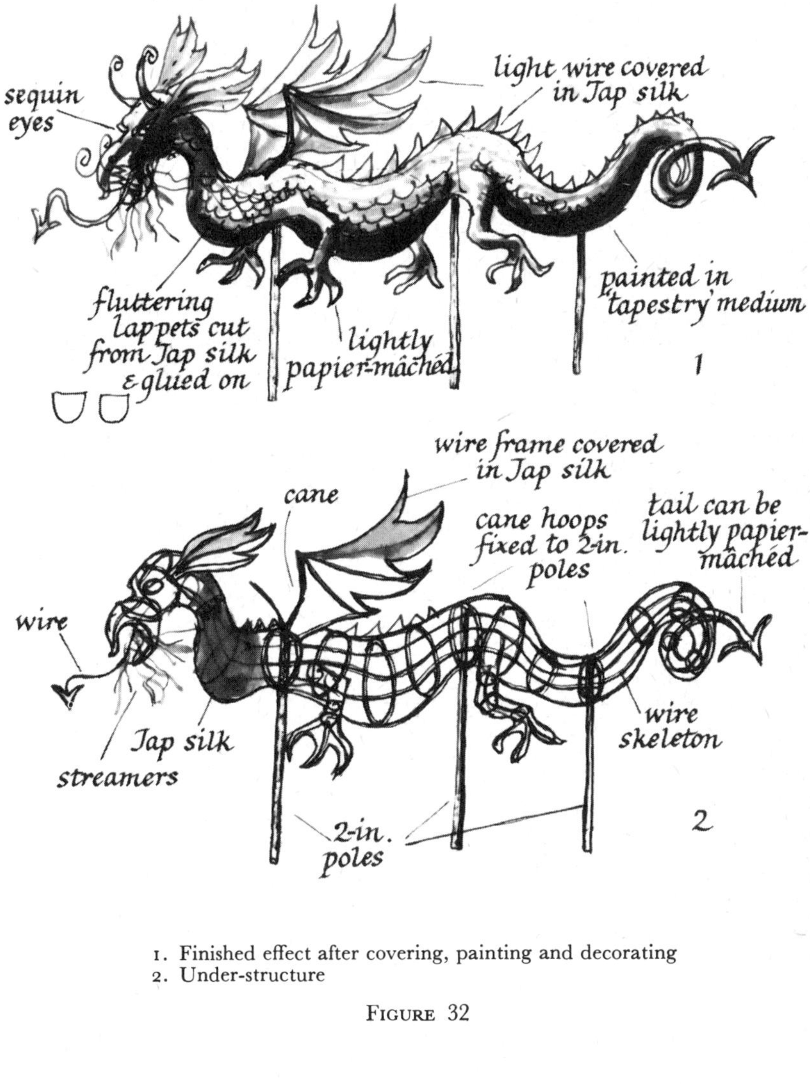

1. Finished effect after covering, painting and decorating
2. Under-structure

Figure 32

COCKEREL

MAKE the head, legs, and body from galvanized wire, stuff the shape with paper and cover with papier mâché. Use real feathers, or metallic foil papers or felt cut out into bands of feather shapes, and glue (Copydex) them in overlapping layers, working from the tail towards the head. Make the comb of felt, stick on glass or sequin eyes and work-up the feet by binding the wire with glue-soaked tape to make it knobbly. If the feathers are made of felt, stiffen them first by soaking with shellac and paint. If they are feathers, colour them with sprayed methylated spirit dyes.

Peacocks, lyre-birds, or any other birds can be made in the same way.

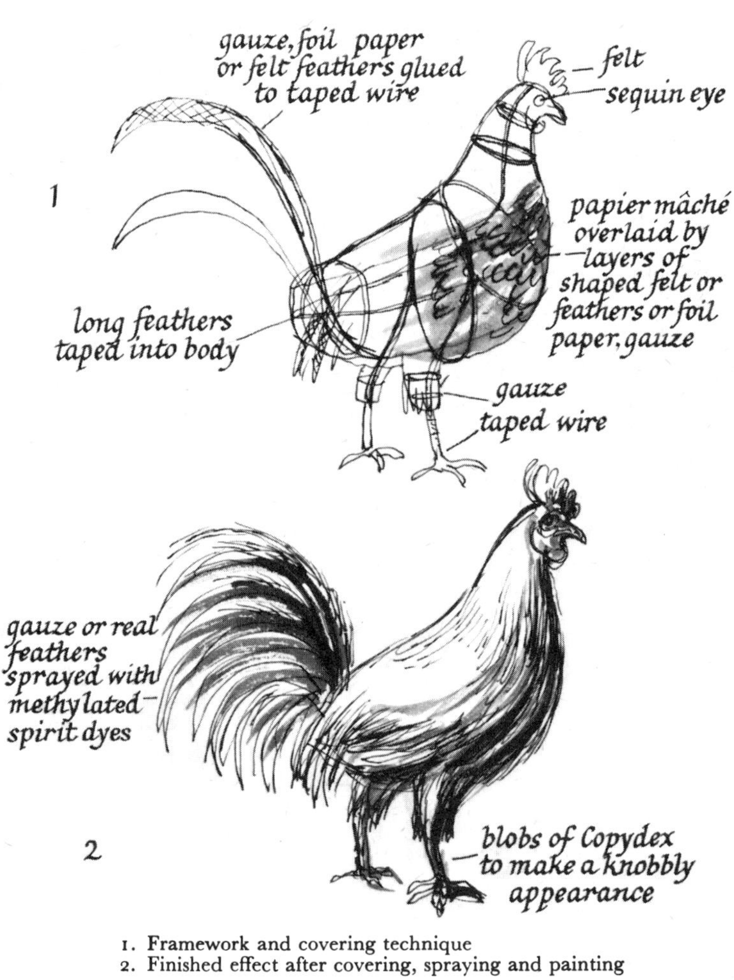

1. Framework and covering technique
2. Finished effect after covering, spraying and painting

FIGURE 33

BUTTERFLY

CONSTRUCT the framework of the wings out of taped galvanized wire. Cover this with taut gauze glued round the taped wire and to itself. Paint coloured area in with dyes (a mouth-spray can be used for this) and stick on shapes of velvet. Brush on paste and sprinkle on sequins and glitter liberally, gently shaking off the surplus glitter. The wings are attached to the tough close-grained mahogany or teak body by means of wire roots pushed through drilled holes. The legs, head, and abdomen are also made of taped wire protruding from the wooden base. The whole is painted with french-enamel varnish and decorated with glitter, sequins, iridescent transparent paper, Cinemoid, and animal baize.

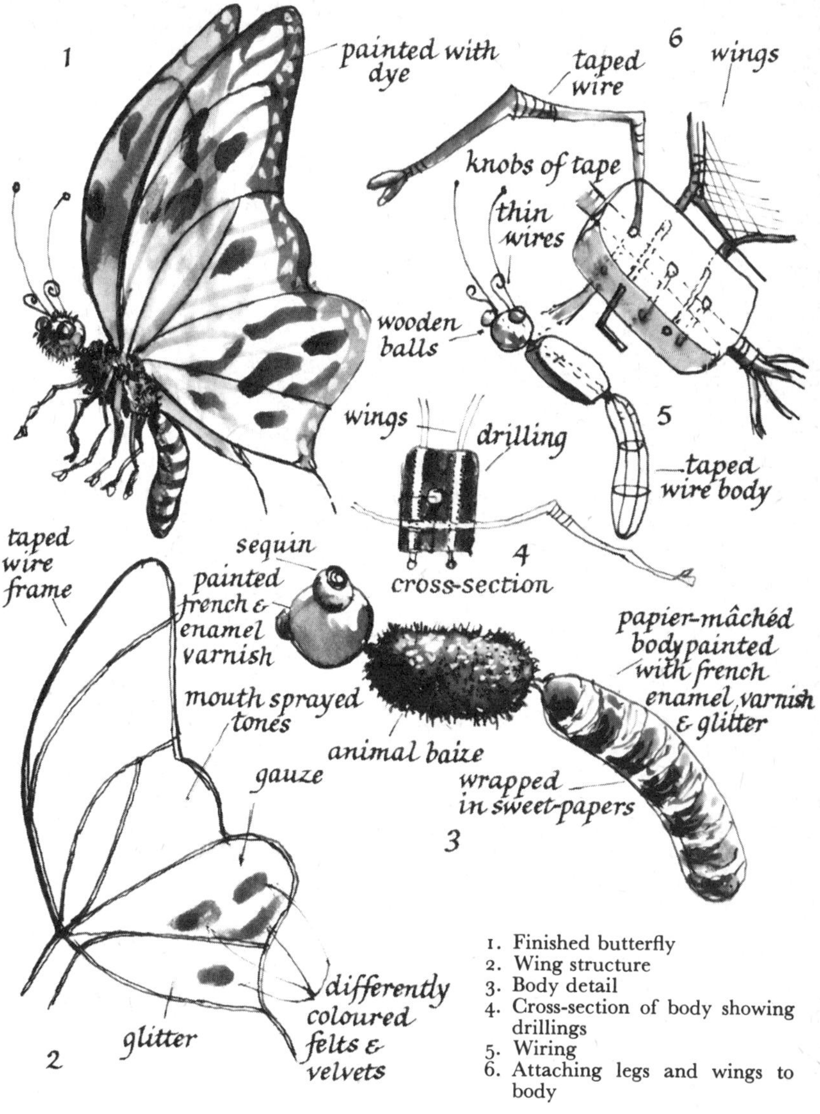

1. Finished butterfly
2. Wing structure
3. Body detail
4. Cross-section of body showing drillings
5. Wiring
6. Attaching legs and wings to body

Figure 34

WINGS AND WANDS

ANGELS' wings are made of a light galvanized-wire frame covered with cloth and feathers glued on in overlaying sequence, finished with white gauze smoothing over the leading edge. The harness can be made of elastic straps taped securely into the wire of the wing frame or a simple device hooking on to the costume.

Fairies' wings are also made of a taped galvanized-wire frame, but covered with taut gauze sprinkled with glitter and sequins (*see* "butterfly"). The harness is made as above.

The wand is a length of dowelling with a battery and press-switch taped to the bottom with the thin flex twisting round and up the wand to the bulb taped to the top. The decoration is of iridescent transparent papers and Cinemoid wired, twisted, and taped to the wand.

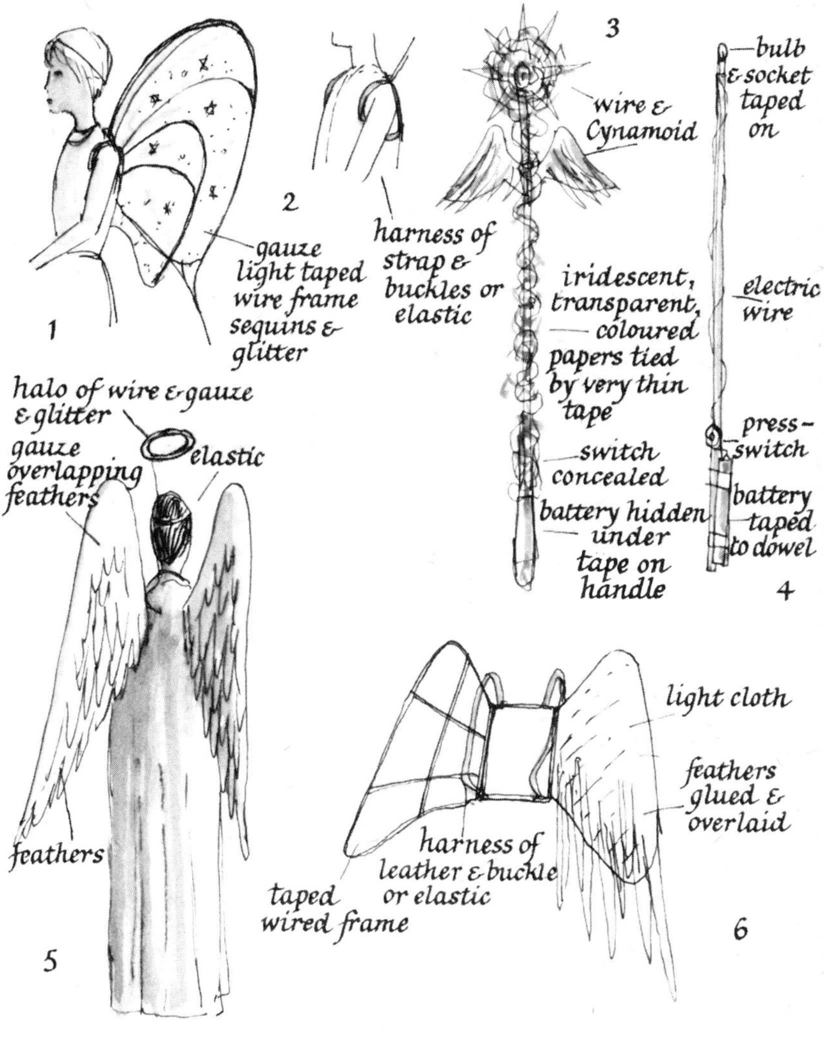

1. Fairy wings
2. Harness
3. Wand
4. Wiring of wand
5. Angel's wings
6. Structure

FIGURE 35

STRINGED INSTRUMENTS

To make a construction in wood, fret out the back and front of the instrument in three-ply and after cutting and carving the neck and head, place wood blocks of the correct thickness between the two flats and pin and glue together. Round the open edge glue and pin skin-ply, felt, or chicken-wire. Where necessary cover with papier mâché, and build up the carved surfaces. When they are dry, decorate the edges with felt and treat the whole instrument with shellac. The knobs, frets and bridges can be made of wood or ply and the strings of thread or cord, stapled, pinned, or glued.

Where a taped-wire framework is used, build up the shape and lash it to the three-ply flat surface, if there is one, by sewing with fuse-wire. Cover the fuse-wire knots on the outer surfaces of the instrument with papier mâché or card. Papier-mâché the framework with carpenter's glue and brown paper torn into little pieces. In the lutes, a fine effect of ribbing will result after they are painted with shellac. The arched bows are made of thin cane or willow heated and bent. Dowelling is used for straight bows with the end-pieces screwed and glued on, with hemp locked under a bar of felt or wood.

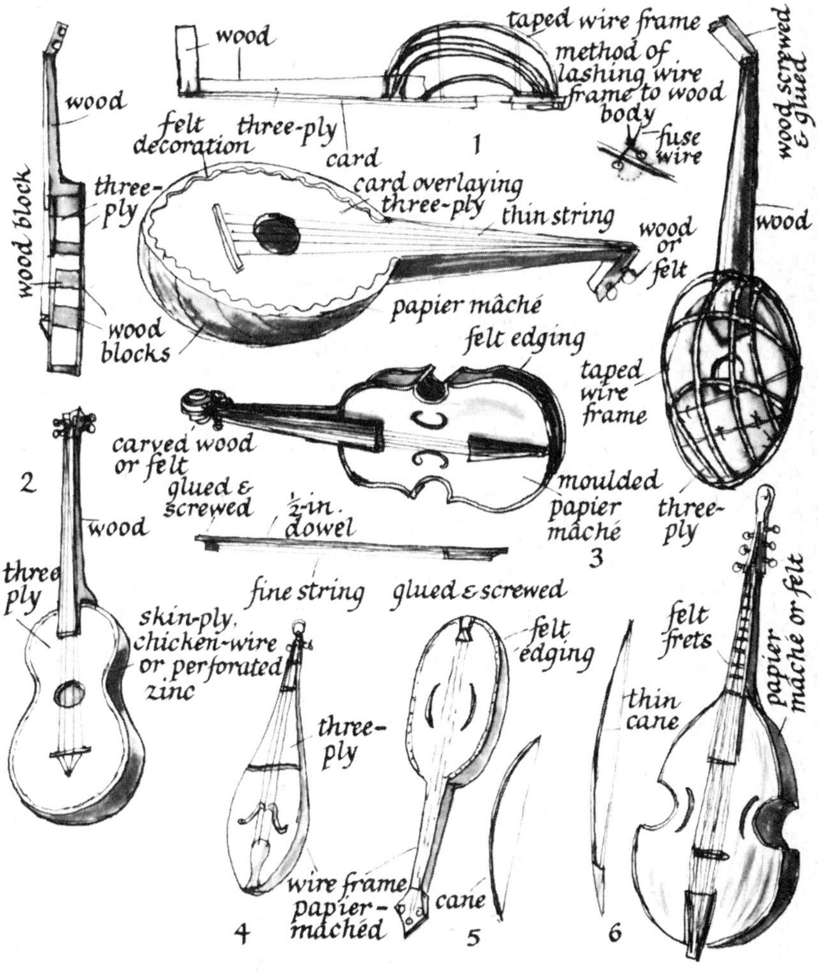

1. Structure of lute
2. Structure of guitar
3. Violin
4. Sixteenth-century rebec
5. Twelfth-century viola
6. Sixteenth-century viola da gamba

FIGURE 36

TRUMPETS AND HARPS

CONSTRUCT the framework of your trumpet or horn of wire, making sure that it is fairly rigid and well shaped. Stuff with screwed-up paper to just below the opening of the mouth, giving an effect of hollowness. Papier-mâché with small pieces until a smooth surface has been attained and when this is thoroughly dry paint it with three or four coats of shellac. Paint again when dry with brass powder in shellac and glaze up until it becomes quite metallic. The mouth-piece can be made of an old kettle-knob taped in, or just of a knot of tape round a wood block fixed into the trumpet's end.

Making harps and lyres is a simple carpentry problem of fretted shapes glued and screwed together with carved components. The strings are glued, tied or stapled in place and the decoration is of felt worked-up with paint, glaze, and metallic foils.

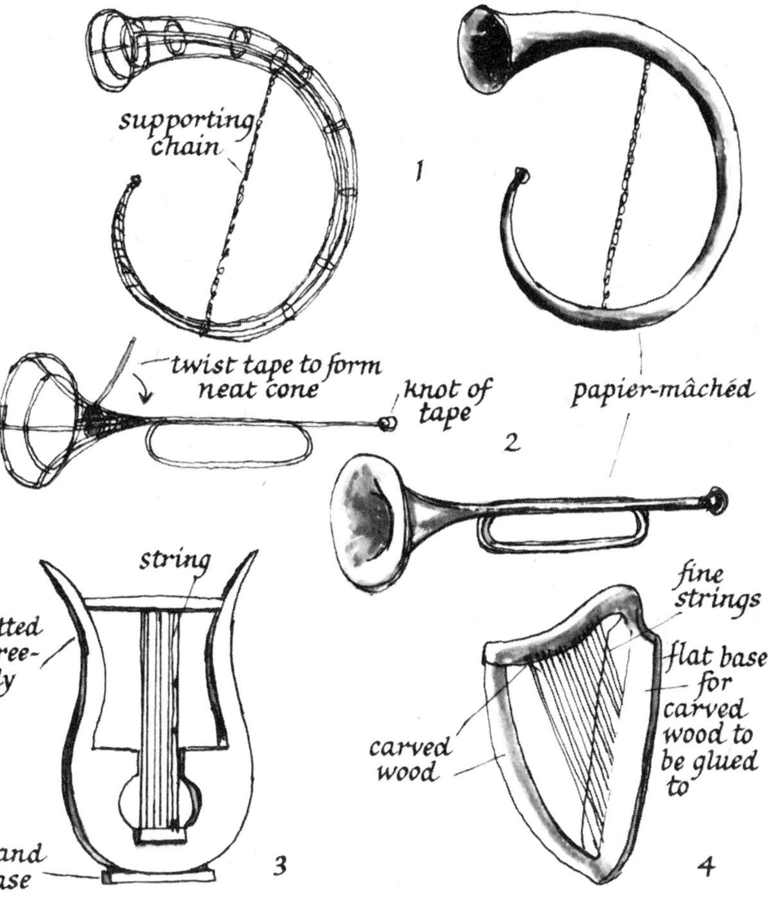

1. Roman horn and structure
2. Trumpet and structure
3. Lyre
4. Harp

FIGURE 37

CROSS-BOWS AND LONG-BOWS

Both bows are easily made by following the drawings. The mechanism for the cross-bow can be omitted. The quiver is either of felt sewn and shellac-stiffened or is papier-mâchéd on a wire frame. The arrows are of dowelling spliced and feathered.

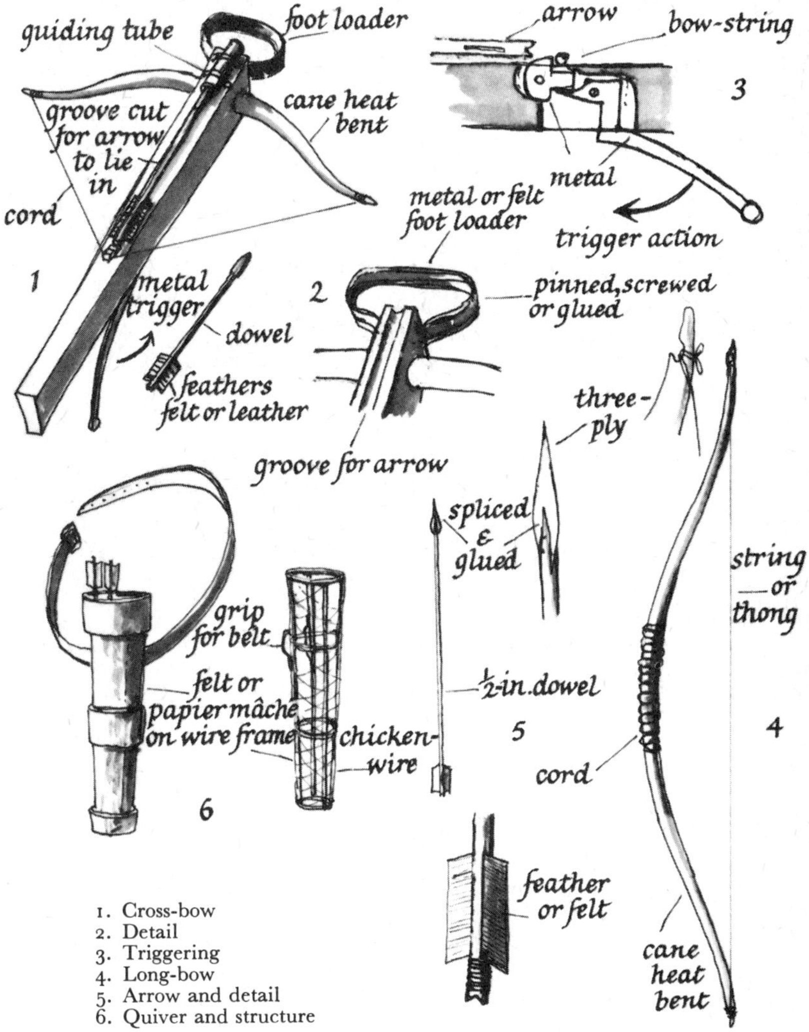

1. Cross-bow
2. Detail
3. Triggering
4. Long-bow
5. Arrow and detail
6. Quiver and structure

FIGURE 38

SHIELDS AND SPEARS

Shields can be made of skin- or three-ply pinned to wooden formers, with straps of leather and decoration of felt, papier mâché, cloth, and paint.

Spears, pikes and pole-axes are made of one-and-a-half-inch poles, spliced and with three-ply blades set in to them (with glue and screws), or of taped-wire frames that can be worked-up with papier mâché and metallic pigments in shellac.

For an old, tattered flag, make a brand new one of canvas and put it into a smoky coal fire for a moment. A centuries-old blackened banner will emerge.

A lance can be made of chicken-wire moulded on discs set along a two-inch tapered pole, papier-mâchéd and painted.

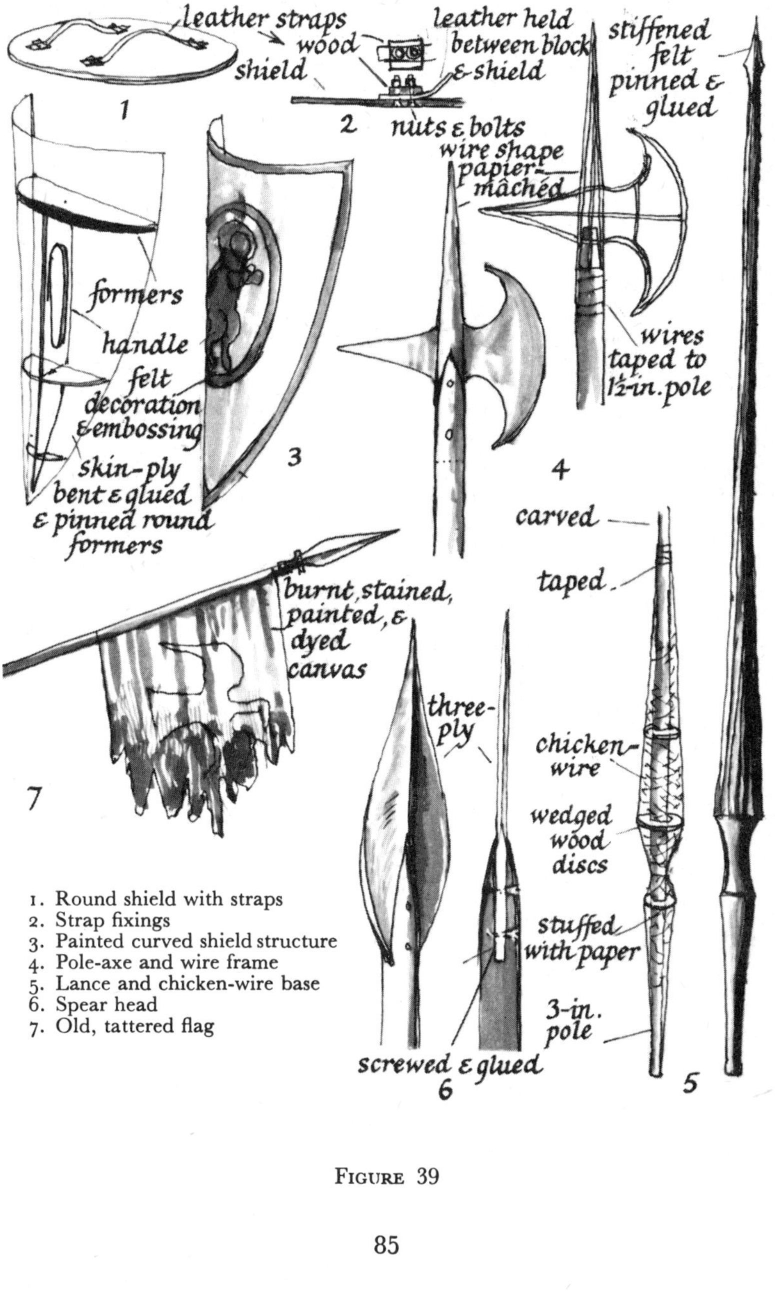

1. Round shield with straps
2. Strap fixings
3. Painted curved shield structure
4. Pole-axe and wire frame
5. Lance and chicken-wire base
6. Spear head
7. Old, tattered flag

FIGURE 39

SWORDS AND SCABBARDS

BROAD-SWORDS, whether Roman, Greek or medieval, are made of a one-piece carved-wood blade and handle, with screwed and glued wooden or felt hilts. The pommels can be of screwed and glued wood or felt, and the handle decorated with twisted glued cord or tape. To make sixteenth- seventeenth- and eighteenth-century complex sword handles, guards and pommels, built-up taped wire frames papier-mâchéd will work quite well. The jewellery and decoration are of felt, sequins, glitter, and metallic foils. The metallic parts are first painted black, and are then painted with silver powder in shellac, worked-up into the appearance of steel with a final glazing.

The scabbard can be made of a felt envelope folded and glued with an overlapping tab. Inside, at top and bottom are wooden shape-formers with an aperture in the upper one for the sword blade to pass through. The whole assembly is strengthened with additional binders of felt and four or five soakings of shellac. The belt is incorporated by simply sewing loops to appropriate hanging points before the shellac is applied. Another method is to make a taped-wire frame with oval loops top and bottom and cover this with papier mâché over glued or sewn buckram.

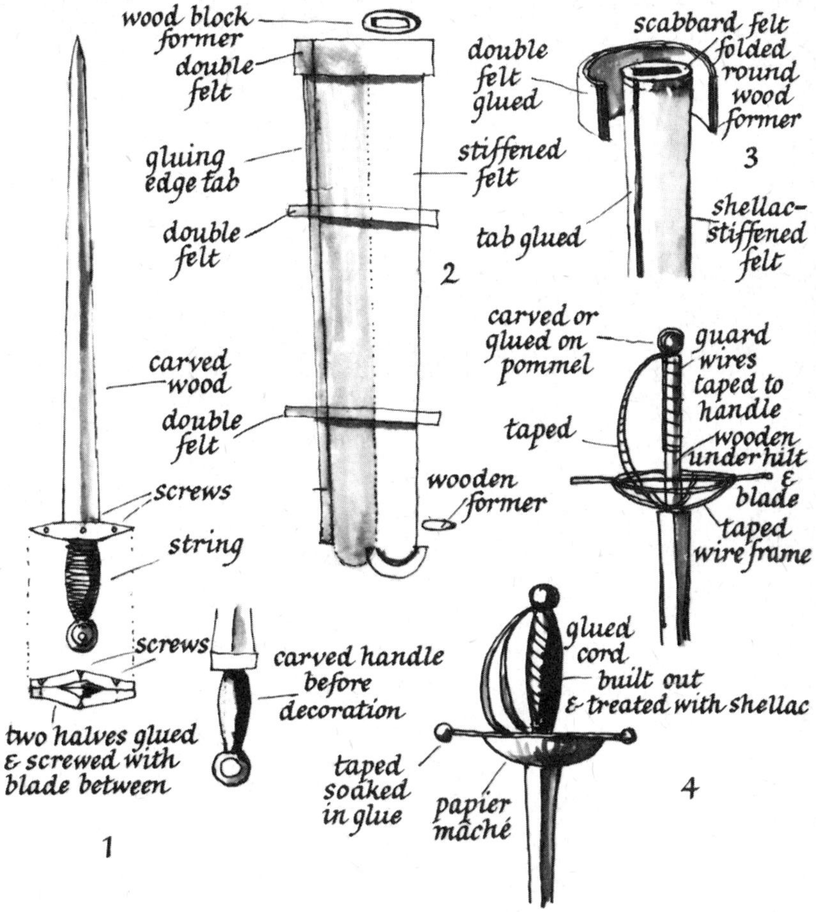

1. Broad-sword
2. Scabbard of felt
3. Detail of binding
4. Rapier guard

FIGURE 40

FIREARMS

ALL firearms are built on the same principle, each has a stock, butt, barrel, and firing-lock. The stock and butt can be made of shaped block-board, ply, or carved timber, with the barrel of drilled dowelling pinned and glued to it. The lock, whether hammer, flint, bolt, match or wheel, is constructed of glued components and the decorations, trigger-guard and barrel-fastenings of shellac-stiffened felt. To give the appearance of gun-metal, paint all the metallic parts black and then, with silver and black mixed in shellac, work-up the shine and glint.

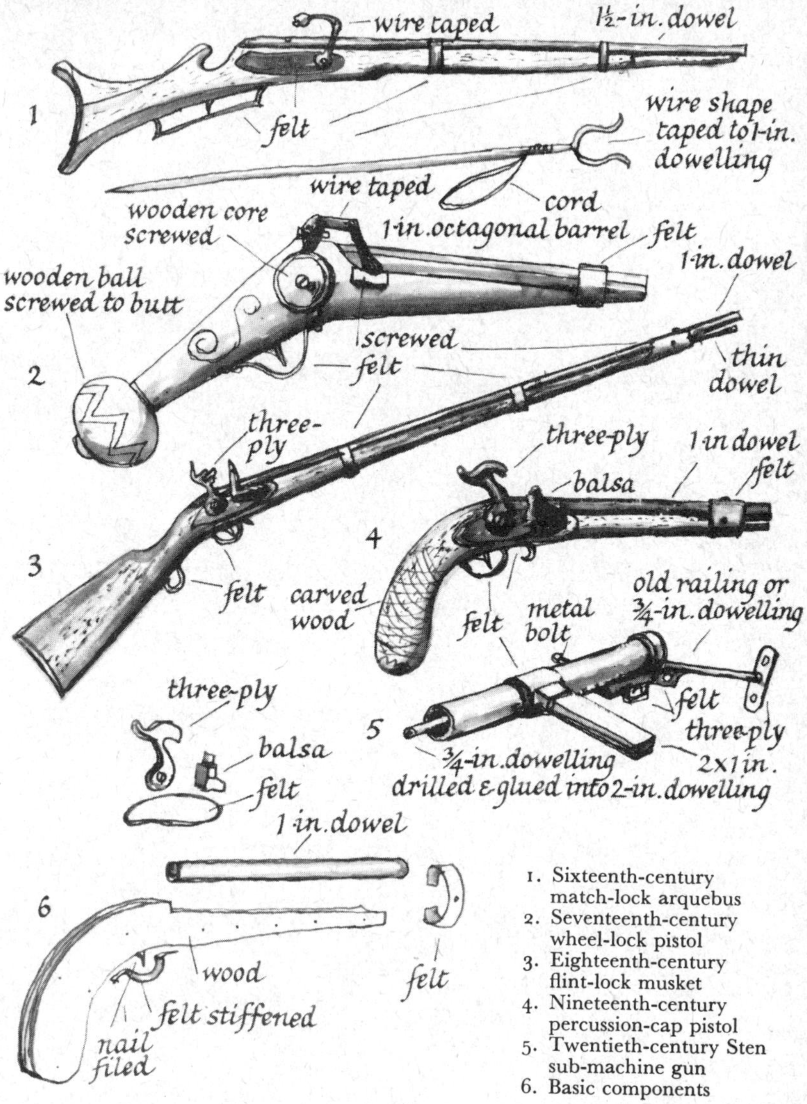

1. Sixteenth-century match-lock arquebus
2. Seventeenth-century wheel-lock pistol
3. Eighteenth-century flint-lock musket
4. Nineteenth-century percussion-cap pistol
5. Twentieth-century Sten sub-machine gun
6. Basic components

Figure 41

CANNON, BANDOLIER, AND POWDER-HORN

BUILD the gun-carriage out of ply or block-board with a set of old wheels, covering the spokes with felt or ply. Construct formers in the shape of the gun-barrel and cover with chicken-wire and papier mâché, finishing with shellac-stiffened felt ridges. Paint the undercoat in black and overlay with bronze or silver metallic pigment mixed with black and shellac.

The seventeenth-century bandolier is a belt hung with hollow wooden cartridges containing powder, wad, and ball. Later bandoliers have pouches for clips of cartridges or leather loops for single rounds, made of shaped dowelling painted with brass powder in shellac.

The powder-horn is made of a wire frame covered with papier mâché and decorated with shellac-stiffened felt. Note the eyelets for the carrying cord; these are bound on the wire frame before the papier mâché is applied.

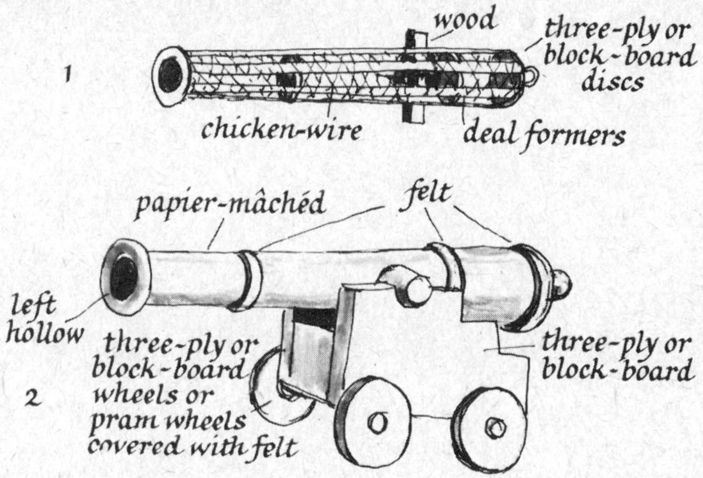

1. Formers and chicken-wire frame of barrel   2. Gun set on carriage

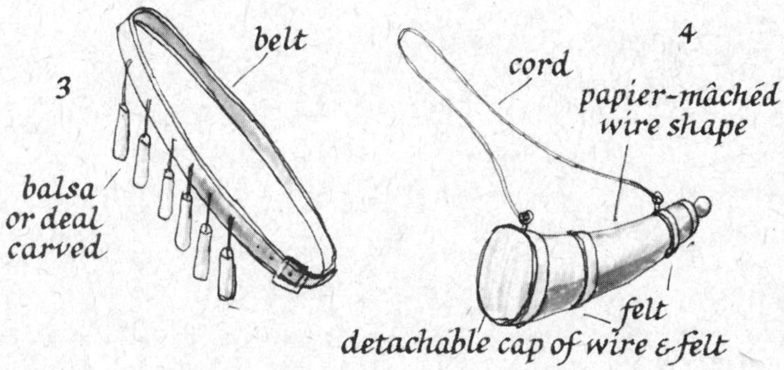

3. Bandolier   4. Powder-horn

FIGURE 42

ARMOUR

PLATE armour can be made of papier mâché on a frame of chicken-wire and galvanized wire, or tailored felt stiffened with size, or better, shellac. Both types need to be modelled on the actor initially, to get the correct fullness and ease. Do not forget the inside padding of soft felt. The torso should be made in two halves and (like all attached sections) be joined by buckles and straps, press studs or hooks and eyes or lacing, or even elastic. Careful examination of a real suit of armour will indicate many points of construction. Remember, too, that sometimes only part of a suit need be worn, e.g. the front half of the breast-plate is often enough if the actor's back is covered by a cloak.

To paint a suit of armour first lay-in with black and cover this with metallic pigments mixed in shellac.

Chain-mail can be made of knitted string painted with black and metallic pigments mixed in shellac. Alternatively make a suit of cloth and sew curtain-rings on here and there, painting the rest to match.

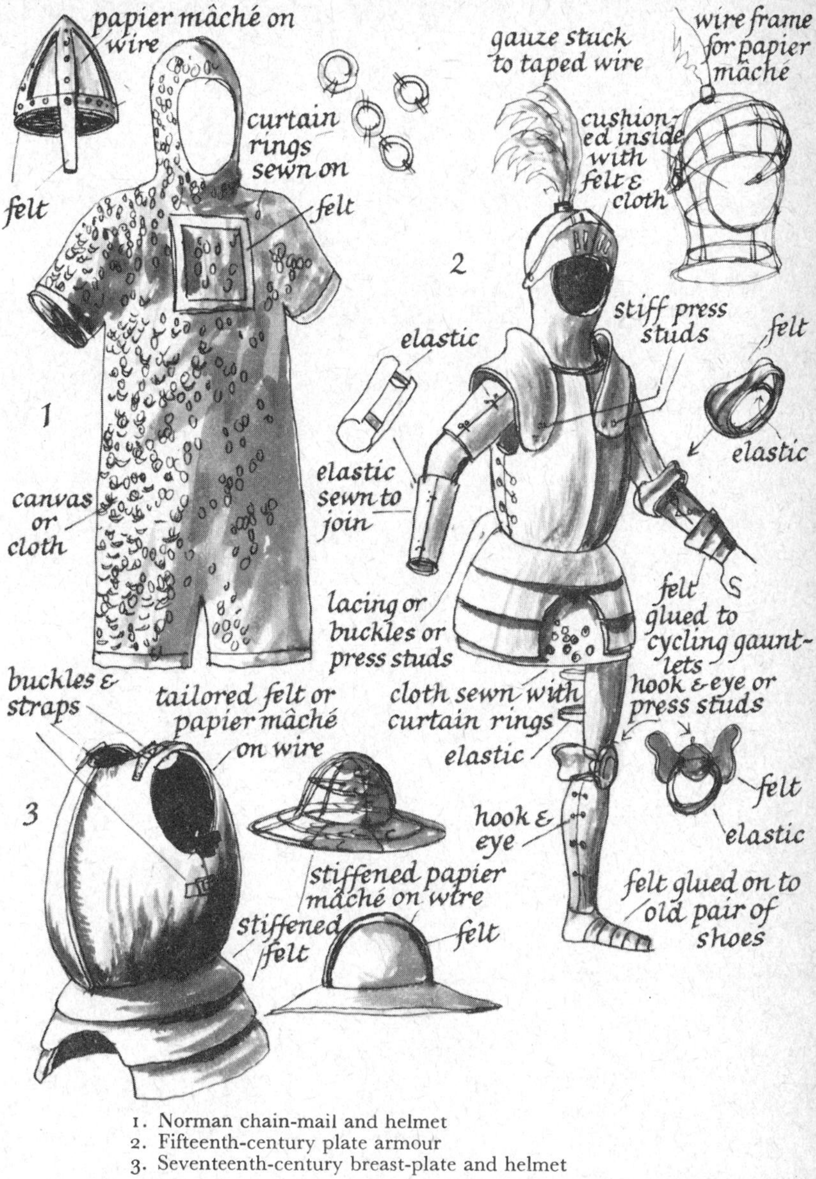

1. Norman chain-mail and helmet
2. Fifteenth-century plate armour
3. Seventeenth-century breast-plate and helmet

FIGURE 43

CLASSICAL MILITARY EQUIPMENT

A Roman centurion's armour can be made of papier mâché on a galvanized wire and chicken-wire frame, or in tailored felt stiffened with shellac or size; for both types use felt padding inside. The decoration is built-up of pulped papier mâché and felt mouldings with stage jewellery embossings. Ordinary soldier's armour was just made of leather, and this can be made of stiffened felt, but painted in leather colours. On metallic areas use metallic pigment in shellac on a black grounding.

Helmets, both Greek and Roman, are based on a papier-mâchéd wire cap with felt and wood attachments sewn or bound in with thin fuse-wire. Plumes can be of gauze, felt, or feathers.

A standard-bearer's head-dress can be made of tailored felt with spots of dye for patterning. The standard is a pole decorated with cut felt shapes, moulded and hardened with shellac, attached to taped wire; wooden cut-outs are screwed to the pole.

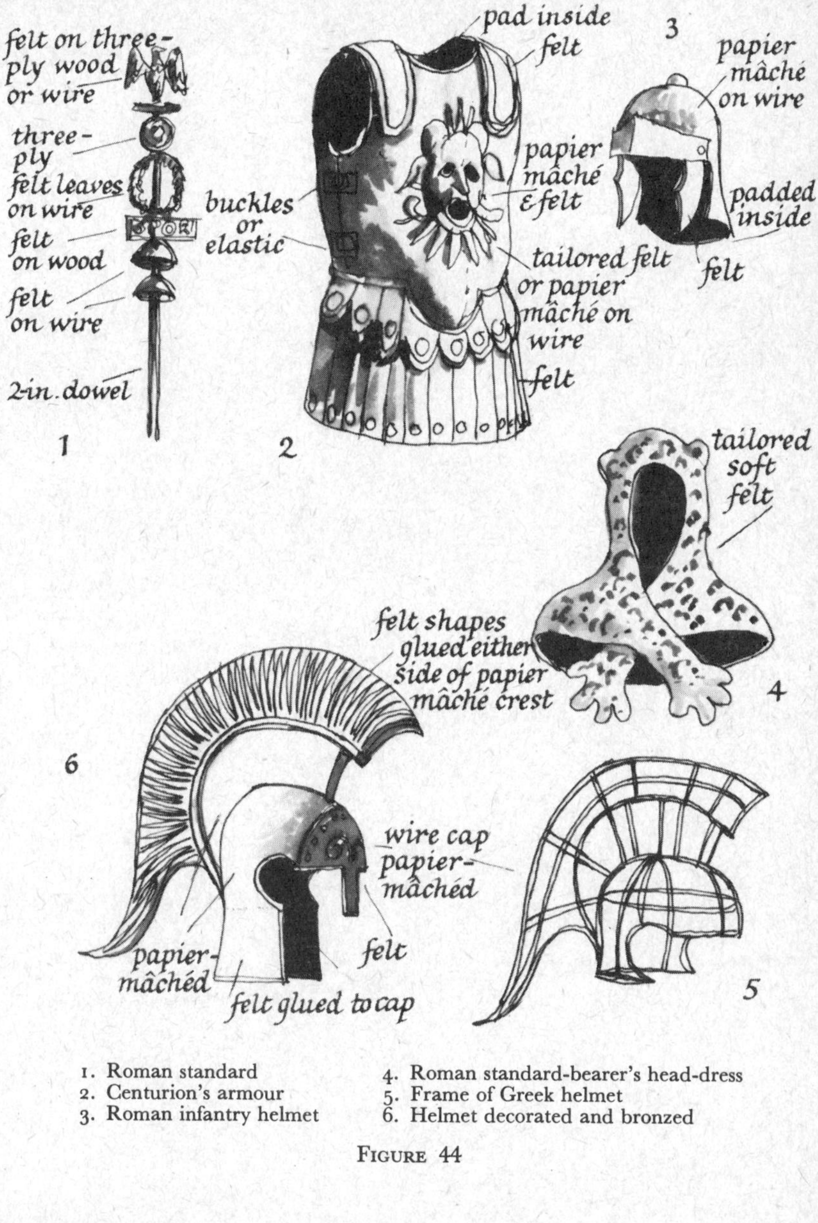

1. Roman standard
2. Centurion's armour
3. Roman infantry helmet
4. Roman standard-bearer's head-dress
5. Frame of Greek helmet
6. Helmet decorated and bronzed

FIGURE 44

WIGS

PROFESSIONAL wig-making is a highly skilled and expensive process. But here is a method that is cheap and simple, and quite adequate for the needs of a supporting cast.

First, make from net, gauze or light cloth, or cut from the top of an old hat, a crown to form a tight-fitting skull-cap and dye this the colour of the hair you intend to cover it with.

Buy a hank of Italian plumber's hemp from a hardware store and split this into three or four units, each one will be enough for one wig. Take one length and cut as in the illustration, into two equal halves.

Decide on a mid-hair-line from the top of the crown of the skull-cap to the centre of the forehead, and cover one half-hemisphere with Copydex or glue. Then, placing the cut edge of one half hank of prepared hemp along the side of the midline, press down and around the cap, working from the front to the back. Glue the other side and, placing the cut edge again along the midline opposite the other edge of the parting, repeat the process, moving from the forehead towards the rear again, intermingling the hair and fusing it into one at the back of the head.

Do not comb too much, but rather brush excess hair out by holding up the wig in one hand and striking with a sharp downward movement with the other. When this first grooming is complete, spray the colour (fixative methylated spirit spray) with methylated spirit dye, and then curl with tongs and cut to style, holding the hair in place with lacquer or map varnish and grips. A little sprayed hair-oil will give the hair lustre.

Warning. Dry the wig thoroughly and do not put it near a naked flame at any time.

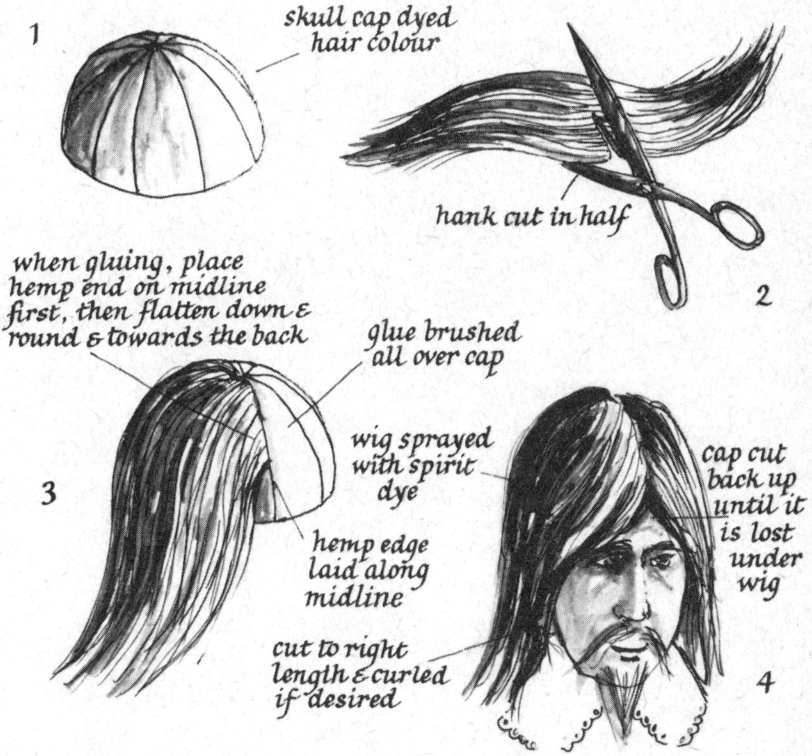

1. Cap
2. Preparing hank of hemp
3. Gluing
4. Colouring, cutting, curling and setting

FIGURE 45

TREES AND TEXTURES OF BARK

Trees can be made of wooden formers and chicken-wired half or full-rounded shapes, or flat-profiled block-board, ply or hardboard built up in relief with papier mâché and felt. The boughs can be made of taped and papier-mâchéd galvanized wire flowing from the limbs of the wooden trunk. Branches are wire continuations of the boughs splaying out into ends of leaves made of canvas, thin felt or leather.

Different trees have different types of bark and these can be imitated very beautifully by using strips of rough felt dipped in hot glue and laid in the characteristic pattern round the trunk. Screwed-up and twisted brown paper soaked in hot glue can also be used with great effectiveness, especially to imitate willow bark and knots.

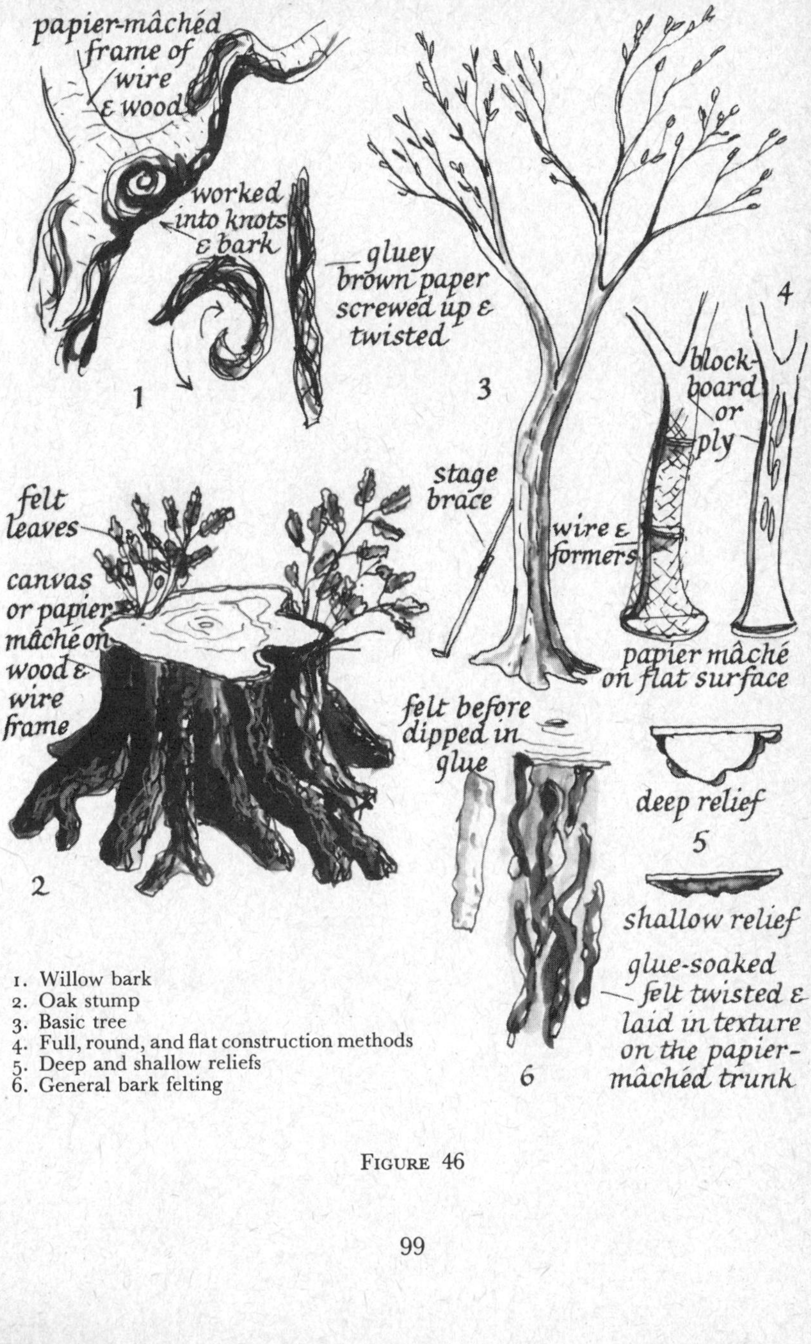

1. Willow bark
2. Oak stump
3. Basic tree
4. Full, round, and flat construction methods
5. Deep and shallow reliefs
6. General bark felting

FIGURE 46

LEAVES

THERE are two techniques for making leaves. One is to glue ready-cut felt shapes to a taped wire or to flower wire, leaving a long end to be taped to the branch. The other method is to glue and fold rectangles of canvas or cloth with taped wire gripped between them. When dry draw the shapes, cut, paint, and tape them into the branches, then into the boughs, finishing on the limbs.

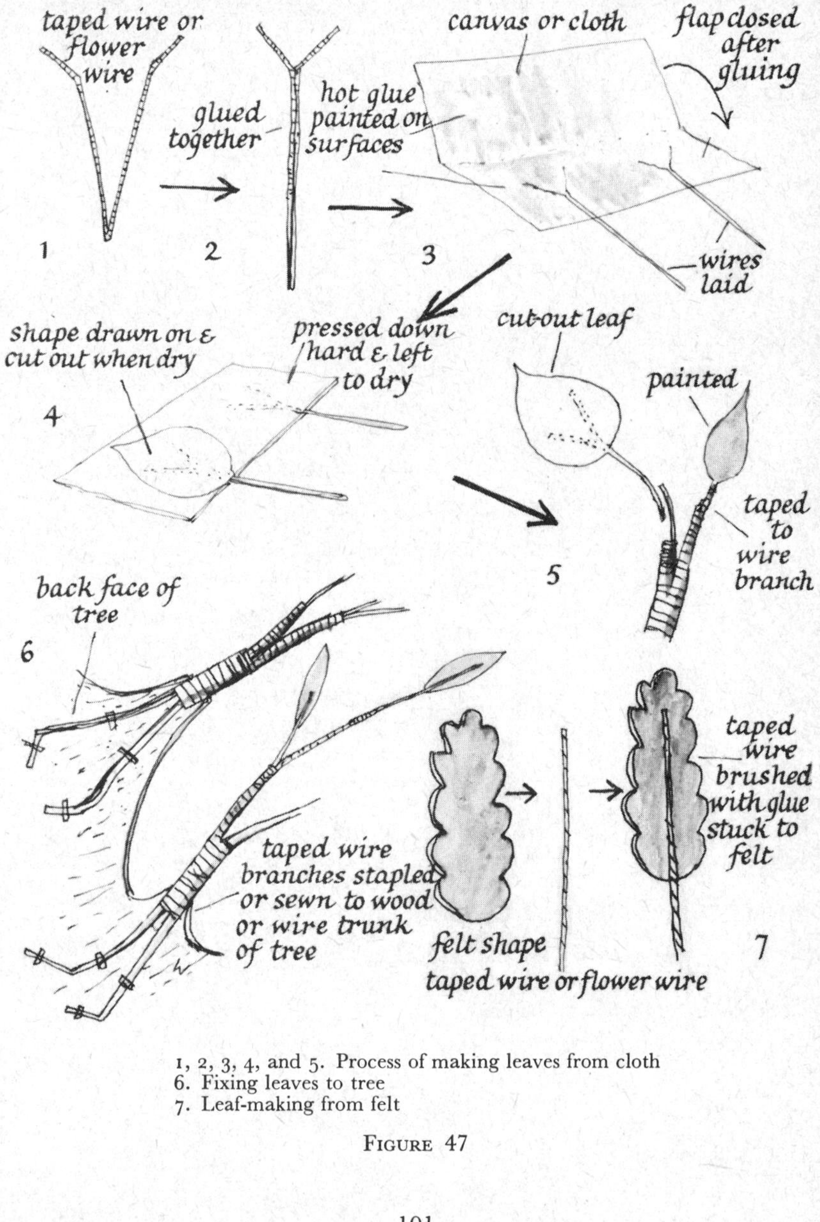

1, 2, 3, 4, and 5. Process of making leaves from cloth
6. Fixing leaves to tree
7. Leaf-making from felt

FIGURE 47

LEAF SHAPES

It is most important that leaves should be the correct shape. Opposite are some specimens of those most used. All of them can be made by using the techniques of taped wire and canvas, felt, leather, or in fact most materials (*see* page 100).

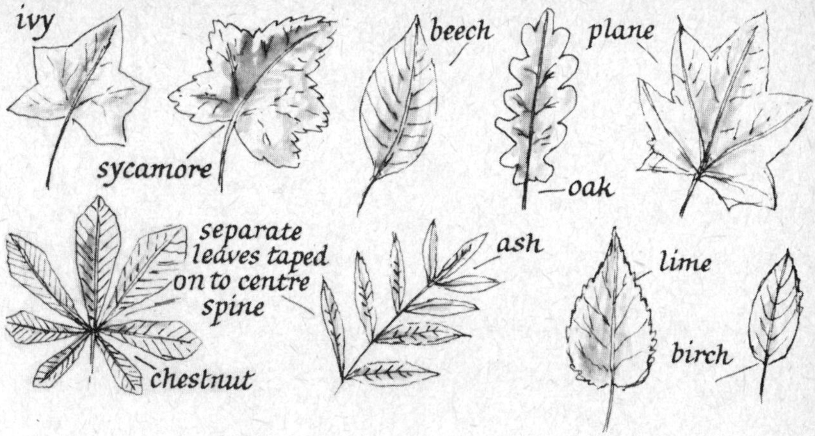

1. English leaves

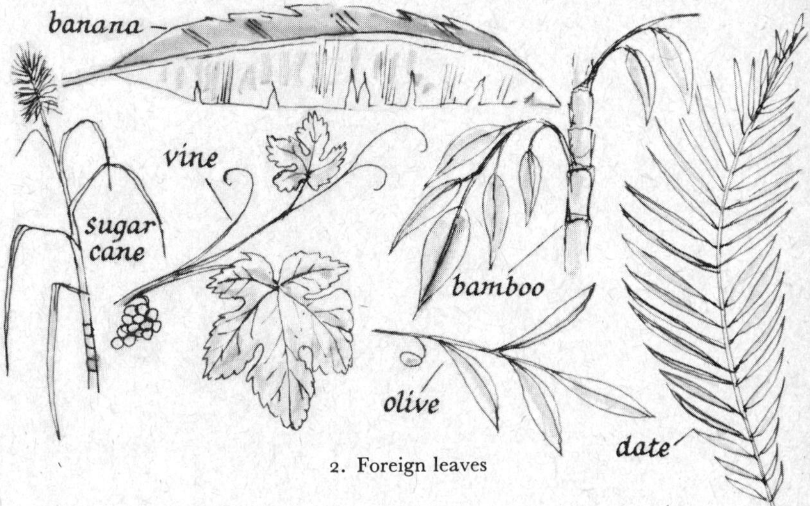

2. Foreign leaves

FIGURE 48

PALMS

After constructing the trunk from formers and applying canvas as described on page 16, cut felt or canvas shapes in bands to be glued round the trunk in overlapping rings. Work from top to bottom marrying them into the base as roots. The leaves are made of folded canvas or of two pieces of canvas glued together with taped wire between. When they are dry, cut to shape, paint and bend, fixing the stem either permanently or detachably into the drilled block set into the top of the trunk.

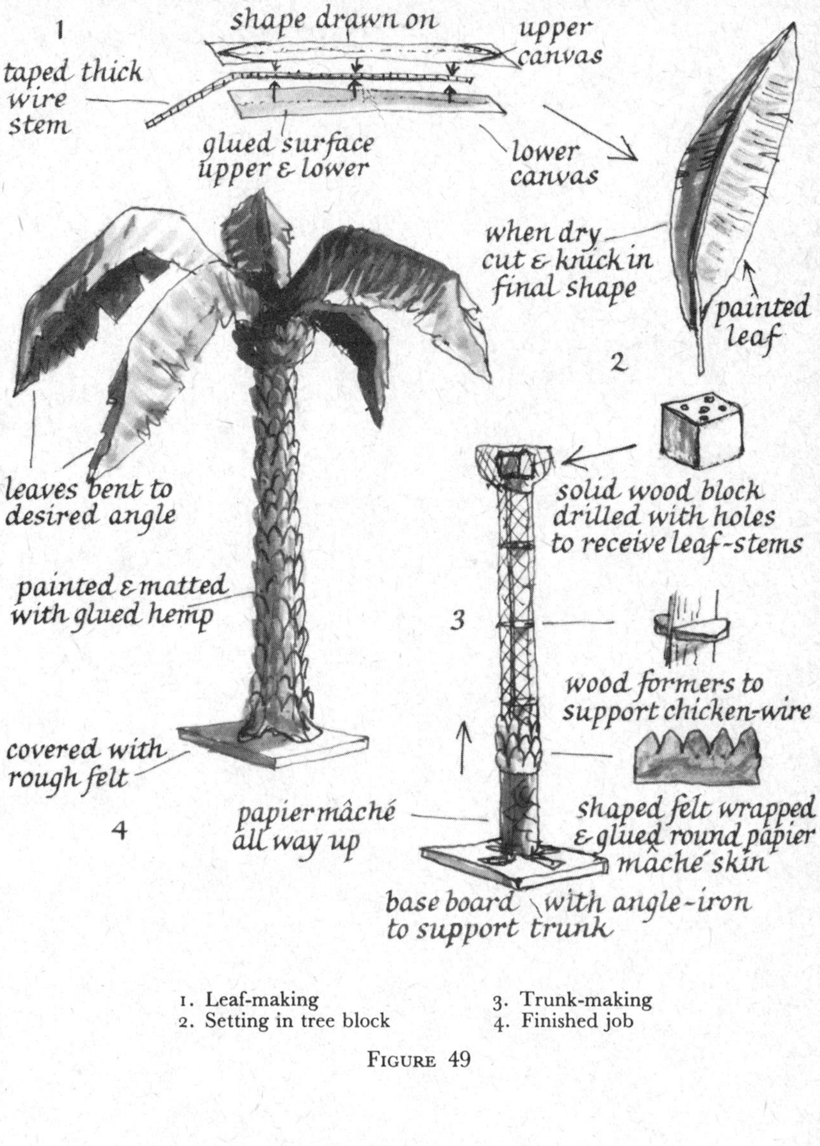

1. Leaf-making
2. Setting in tree block
3. Trunk-making
4. Finished job

FIGURE 49

GROUND ROWS AND POTTED PLANTS

Cut a supported upright shape from hardboard or ply giving it the outline of a bush. Paint on it a background of leaves and shadows. Make long-stemmed branches of taped galvanized wire with canvas or felt leaves. Drill holes in the flat shape and push through the stems, fixing the ends to the back with staples or twisted loops of wire. When the branches are secure, twist and move them about on the face side until with a touch of paint they become one with the flat painted leaves.

Make your plant out of taped galvanized wire, using felt, gauze, canvas, or linen, for the leaves and flowers. After passing the stem through the wooden disc that will make the earth at the top of the pot, knot the wires of the stem into a ball that will fit neatly into the bottom of the pot. Half fill the pot with wet plaster of Paris and set the wire in and hold upright until dry. When the plaster is hard, the plant should stand upright. Glue rough felt to the wooden disc round the stem and paint it to look like earth and moss.

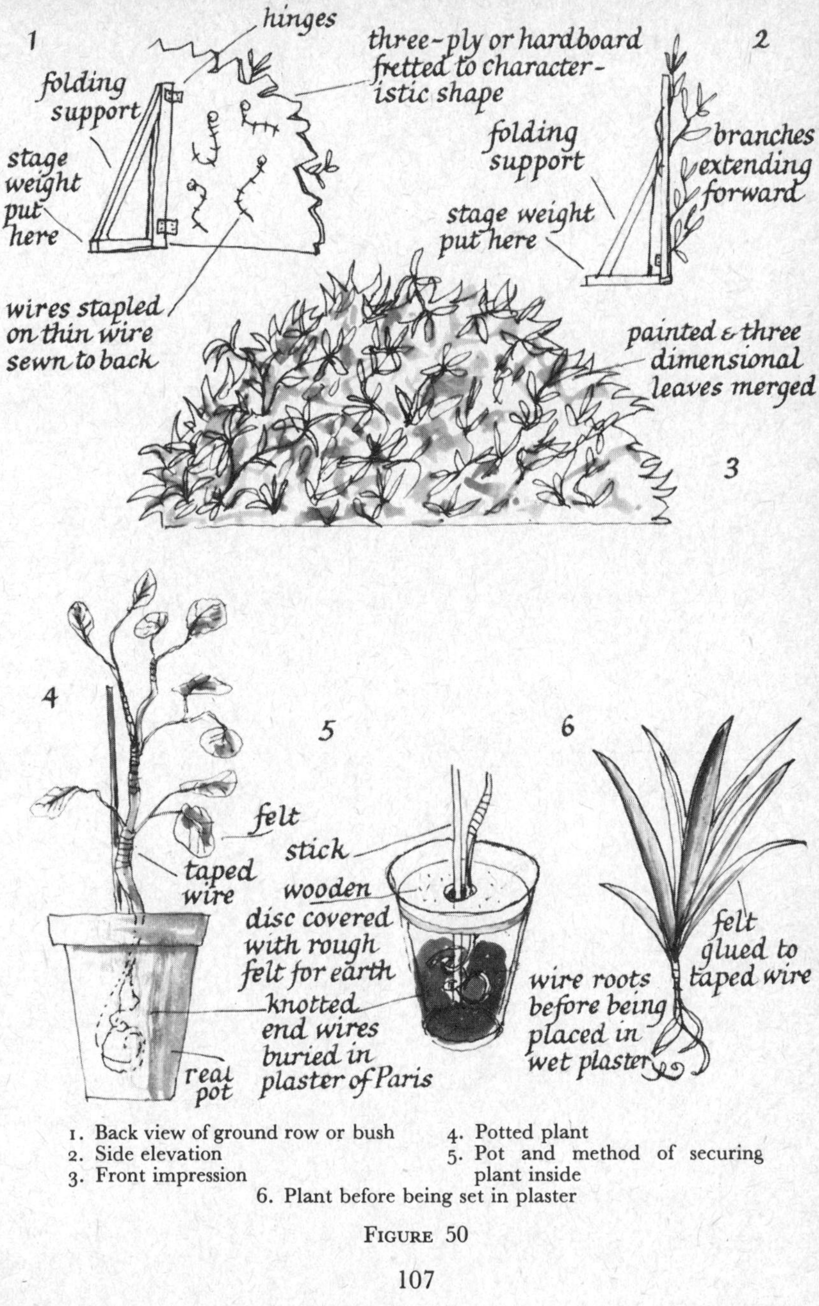

1. Back view of ground row or bush
2. Side elevation
3. Front impression
4. Potted plant
5. Pot and method of securing plant inside
6. Plant before being set in plaster

FIGURE 50

FLOWER-MAKING

THE art of flower-making is delicate and complex, but here are some simple principles that can easily be applied.

Study the species that you wish to make, carefully from an actual plant, photo or drawing. Break down its most characteristic features into basic components, e.g. petal, sepal, stamen, and leaf. Taking the petal as an example, draw the shape using a templet of cardboard on pre-dyed flower linen, or plain linen or canvas, in three sizes, large, medium, and small. Do this with all the components, using felt or canvas for sepals and leaves. Having drawn a sufficient number of units on the materials, cut the shapes out and prepare the stalks. This is done by cutting appropriate lengths of both thick and thin wire, and taping them to give a gluing surface (if cotton-bound flower wire is used this is unnecessary). When the right number have been cut the flower-making can begin. Glue the bases of the petals with Copydex to the top of a thin wire arranging them in their characteristic pattern. After gluing, mould the sepals round their base and spread out the flower into its natural design. Glue the leaves to the wires and tape or glue the flower and leaf stems to the thicker stalks in correct sequence. Build up the plant, binding groups of leaves and flowers into bunches bending and twisting them so that the plant appears to be alive. When the whole plant has been made, spray or paint with methylated spirit dyes, finishing up with a gentle spraying of fire-proofing solution.

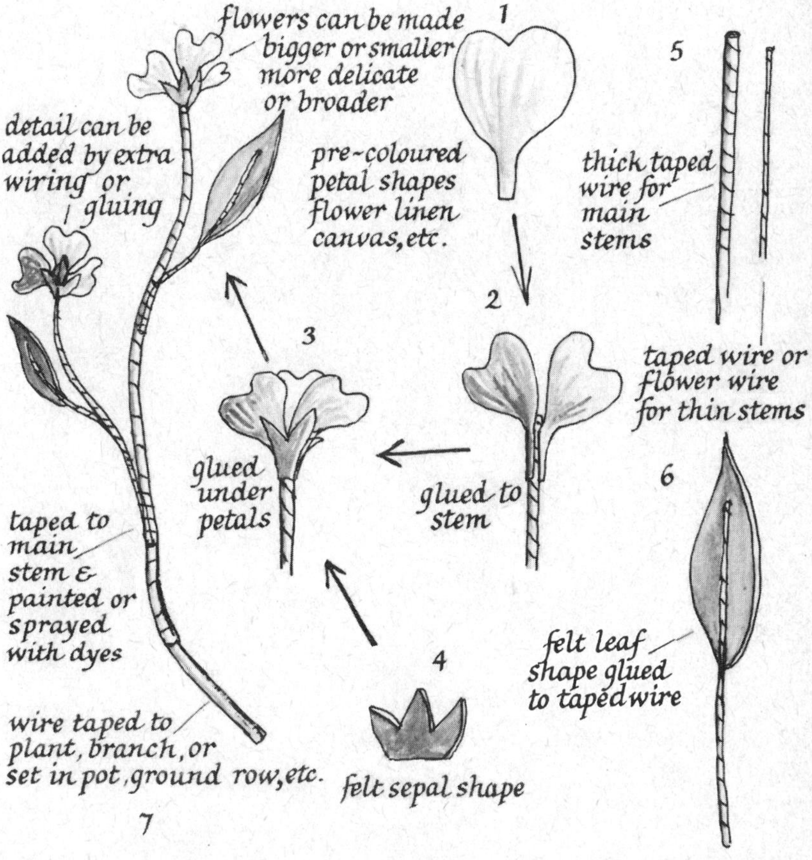

1, 2, 3 and 4. Flower-making process
5 and 6. Stalk- and leaf-making
7. Completed flower

FIGURE 51

FOOD

Most stage food is not to be eaten and can be made of wire frames stuffed with paper and papier-mâchéd and painted. Melons, roast peacocks, chickens, hams, sides of beef, boars' heads, pies, cheeses, cakes, and confections can be made in this way. Sandwiches and biscuits can be made of plywood. For sweets, wood blocks painted and twisted in sweet-papers and foils will do. Plastics, such as foam-rubber, painted, can be used to make slices of ham, cucumber, or tomatoes. Gauze or cotton-wool makes cream for puffs and pastries. Plaster of Paris can be used for many things, such as icing, custards, and creams. Glue-blobs dropped on meat and chickens will give the impression of gravy, and glaze used on paint gives a tasty glisten to both fruit and meat. Plastic fruit can be bought, or papier mâché worked-up carefully will do for apples, pears, oranges, etc. A loaf of bread may be thoroughly dried over a fire and then painted with shellac to save it from going mouldy. Coloured Cinemoid or Cellophane, screwed up or flat, makes jellies, flans and crystallized fruits, or, when wound round painted rods, candy-sticks or rock.

When the food is to be eaten fish and meat can be imitated by mashing bananas and covering with melted chocolate, or potatoes may be used, either boiled or not, and likewise stained with some edible colouring. A fried egg can be made of half an apricot on flour paste.

For drinks, correctly diluted milkless tea will give a fairly accurate coloration for wines and spirits.

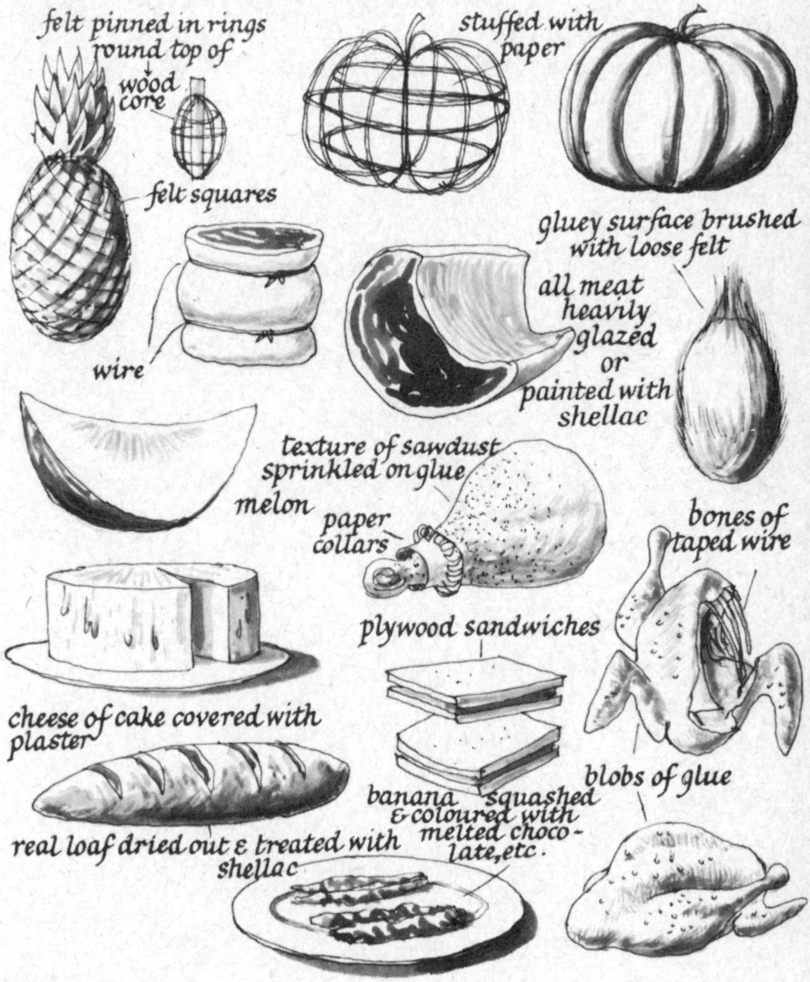

A selection of foods

FIGURE 52

PRINTING AND STENCILLING

To obtain a repeating pattern, such as a bank-note, a lino block should be made. This is done by the process of drawing the image in reverse and cutting out (with lino tools) the white sections of the design, leaving only the raised printing surfaces. Squeeze from a tube of printer's ink the colour required on to a sheet of glass and work the ink backwards and forwards with a roller. When the roller is evenly coated, ink up the block and when it is completely covered, take a sheet of paper cut to size, lay it on the block and work gently over its back with a spoon. Pull the paper off and lay on another and, using the same technique of pressure, find by experiment the right amount of ink and pressure to produce the desired intensity of print. After a few "pulls" the feel will come and a wad of stage notes will soon emerge. For multi-coloured notes or patterns two or three blocks can be cut out and experiments can be made to discover the effect of over- and under-printing the various colours.

Stencilling is another method for reproducing a constant pattern. If stencil paper cannot be obtained, sugar paper stiffened with five or six coats of shellac will do. To make the stencil draw the pattern in reverse (if asymmetrical), cut it out with a very sharp knife and shellac the cut edges to prevent paint corrosion. To print, mix up a stiffish thickness of paint and stencil with a flat thick brush if a stencil brush is not available. Spraying is another method of applying paint to a stencil and spattering with a brush yet another.

When a continuous pattern is being worked, be sure to cut marked notches at key points, so that it is possible to match and continue the flow of the design.

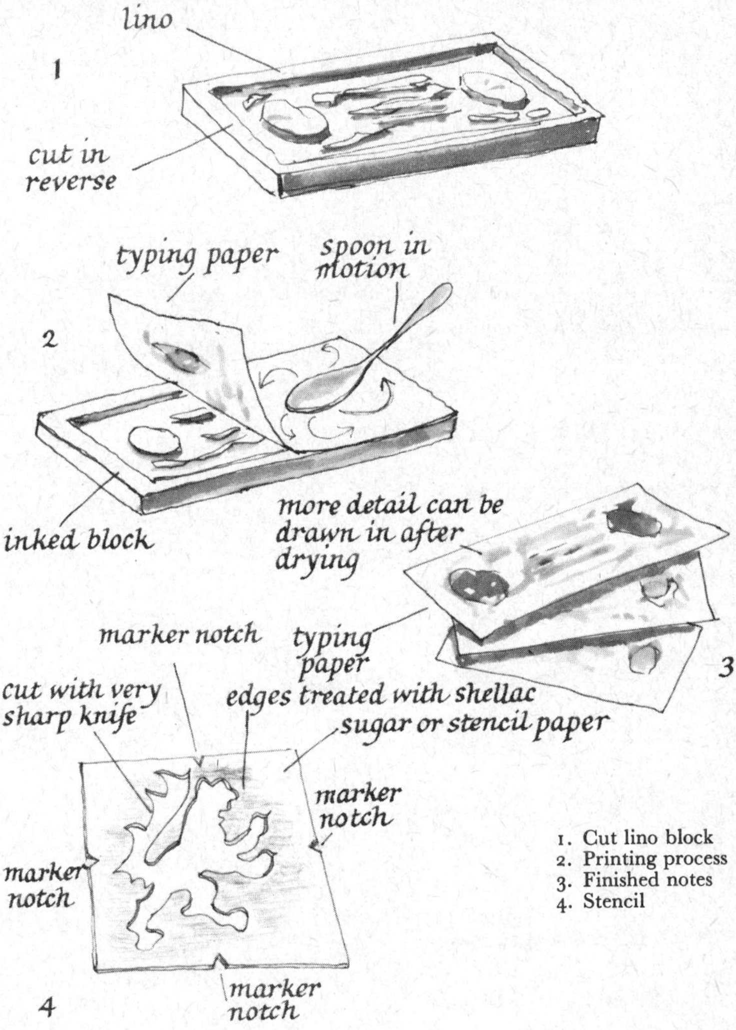

1. Cut lino block
2. Printing process
3. Finished notes
4. Stencil

FIGURE 53

REPRODUCING A POT

SOMETIMES a pair of pots is needed when only one exists. To make a second, a replica of the first, cover the original vase with petroleum jelly and papier-mâché it with two layers of unpasted paper. Follow this with three layers of pasted paper, being careful not to make it too thick and, therefore, much larger than the original when they stand together. Finish off with tissue, and when it is thoroughly dry cut the skin lengthwise in halves to separate from the master pot. Join the two halves together, using elastic bands to hold them temporarily in position, and papier-mâché the joins, removing the elastic bands when the papier mâché is sufficiently strong to bind the pot. Leave to dry, and when ready to give the final binding treat the surface with shellac before painting and glazing.

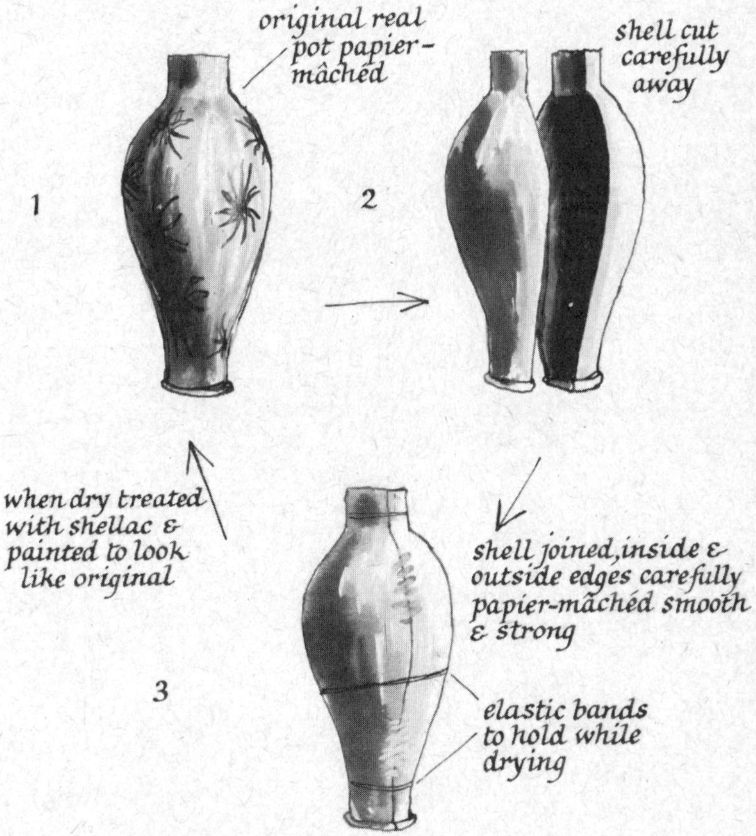

Process of repetition

FIGURE 54

MAKING NEW POTS

ORIGINALLY designed pots can be made to almost any shape with chicken-wire on wood or with galvanized-wire frames. If the wire-frame method is used, rings taped within the modelled uprights are all that will be needed. If, however, wood is used, a length of 2 in. × 2 in. with wooden discs pinned on either end will serve as a good skeleton to hang the chicken-wire on. Cover both frames with papier mâché, working-up details and decoration with felt or pulped papier mâché. Paint this with shellac before finishing with colours and glaze.

Another method of making pots or cups is to have them turned on a lathe, using a templet as the master shape. This produces a very beautiful finish, but is, however, a rather expensive process.

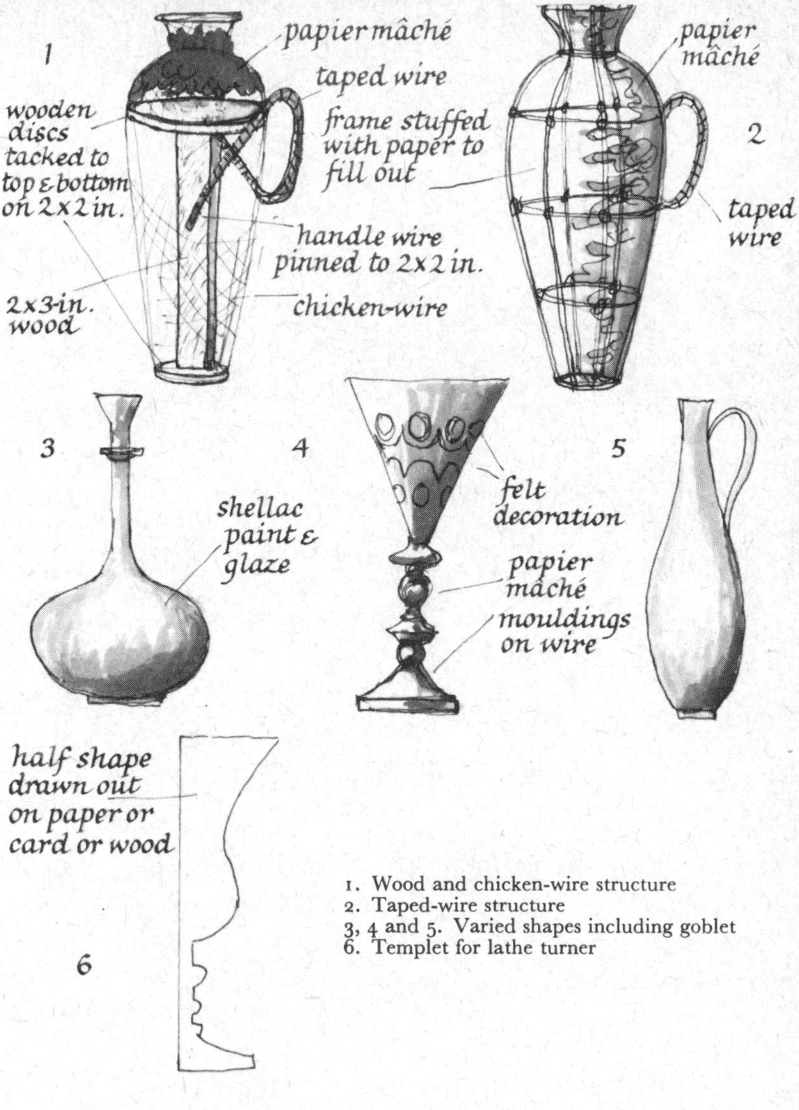

1. Wood and chicken-wire structure
2. Taped-wire structure
3, 4 and 5. Varied shapes including goblet
6. Templet for lathe turner

FIGURE 55

BINDING A BOOK

TAKE the unbound pages and square them up into a block. Measure against this block two squares of hardboard or stiff card. Cut these covers to size, leaving a slight overhang on three sides and a small gap between the inner edge and the spine of the paper block (marked *G* in illustration). Cut from cloth or canvas a shape slightly larger than the area made by two faces of the paper block, plus the width of its spine and the additional outer edge overlap of the hardboard (2). Leaving a space a spine's width plus the gap on either side, shown in (2), glue the hardboard to the canvas, folding the edges over to the inside and covering them neatly with paper (2). Taking the canvas and hardboard unit we now fold the paper block inside (1) and drilling holes through the gap area we insert looped wires and knot them by twisting. To give a more substantial spine glue moulded card along the back and overlay this with carefully glued felt or canvas (3). Decoration is with felt or papier mâché or leather and paint.

The principle of constructing a very large book (say 2 ft × 4 ft) with stiff hardboard pages, that might be used to number acts and scenes is illustrated (4). The method is the same as that already described, except that canvas is glued to the painted hardboard at the bending point.

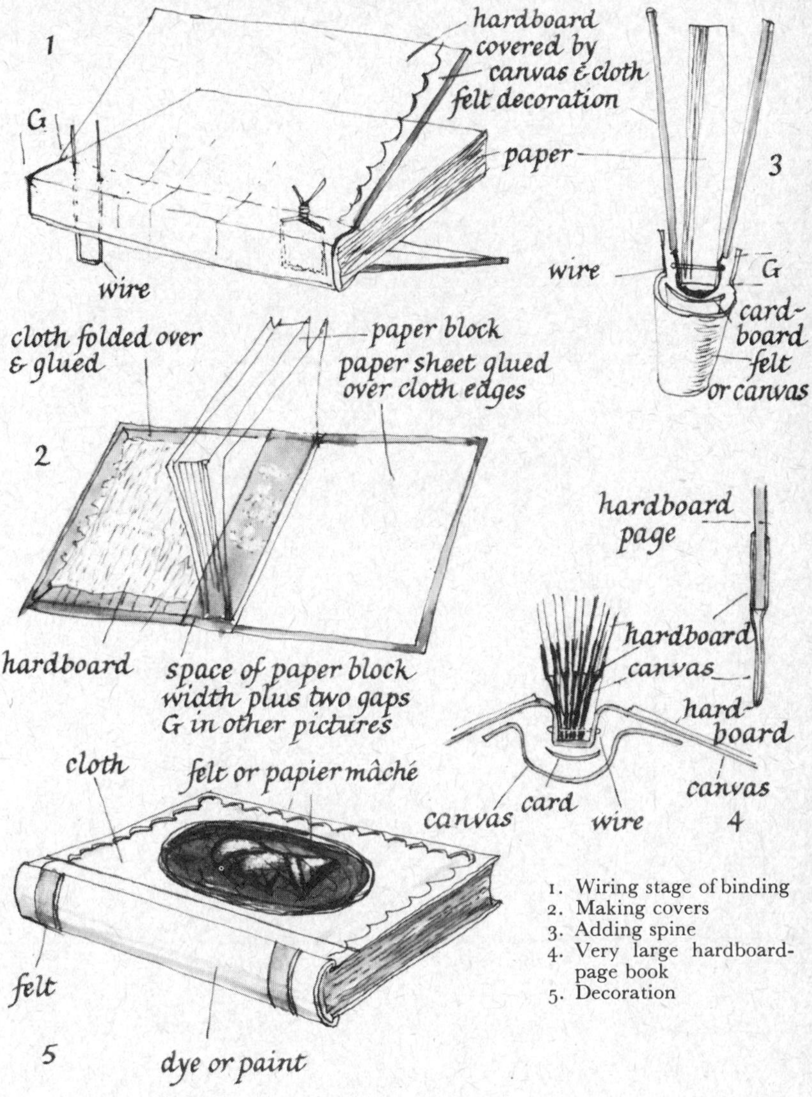

1. Wiring stage of binding
2. Making covers
3. Adding spine
4. Very large hardboard-page book
5. Decoration

FIGURE 56

POLYSTYRENE

POLYSTYRENE (or polystyrene foam as it is known in the U.S.) is a light, firm plastic solid that can be carved into convenient shapes. It can come in solid blocks, but the most common form is to be found in industrial offcuts, or moulded units in packing cases. If a big enough single block cannot be found, then pieces can be joined by gluing and sewing together with wires so as to make a larger mass. Size glue may be used and certain plastic adhesives, provided they do not melt the polystyrene.

When the desired volume is obtained and firmly bound, draw the front, side and top profile on the block, then remove, with a saw or bread knife, the main offcuts. Do not use these tools for delicate or close work, because they rip the plastic rather than cut it. For precise carving, cut with a sharp knife or better a heated one which will easily slice through the plastic until cold. For really delicate work, use a heated wire bent for each cut. Tape the wire so that the heat does not burn the hand. Reheat when cold and it will cut again. Great finesse of detail can be obtained with practice.

Because of its plastic nature polystyrene rejects some paints, especially oil-based ones, therefore it is wise to give it a surface of papier mâché (size glue or paste) paper or canvas, or cover with gauze dipped in some binding agent like plaster or a PVA plastic glue. When dry more detail can be added with papier mâché, and the surface painted; any addition, such as string hair or decorations, can be glued on to a workable surface.

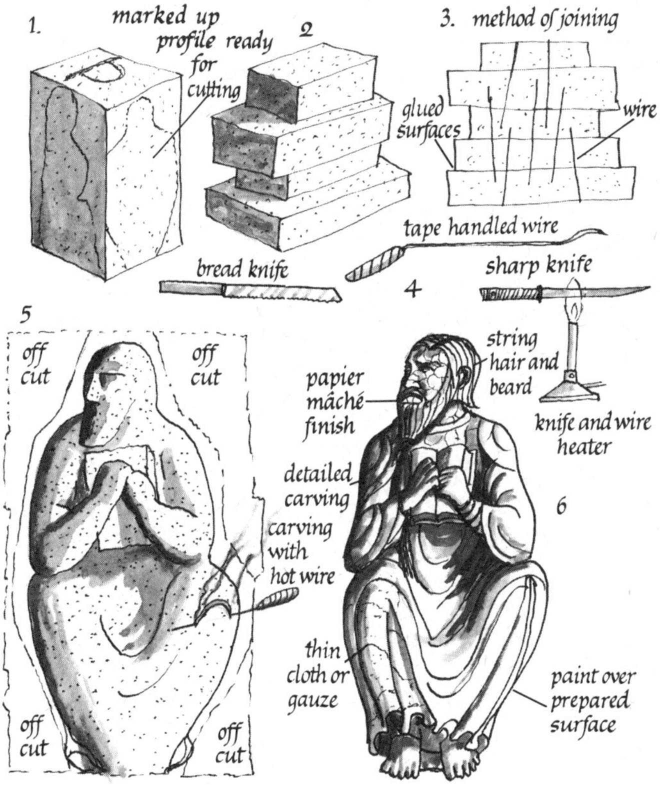
1.
marked up profile ready for cutting
2
3. method of joining
glued surfaces
wire
tape handled wire
bread knife
4
sharp knife
5
off cut
off cut
carving with hot wire
off cut
off cut
papier mâché finish
string hair and beard
knife and wire heater
detailed carving
6
thin cloth or gauze
paint over prepared surface

FIGURE 57

POLYSTYRENE IN COMBINATION

Polystyrene may be used with other materials. In the crab, taped wire is inserted into the main mass of the body and secured by pressing the wires at angles and taping them to their opposites on the far side of the body (be careful not to weaken the fabric of the plastic). The forms on the wire legs may be built up of papier mâché or felt glued to the taped skeleton, or polystyrene sections of the limbs threaded and glued into place. The whole is then papier mâchéd with paper or thin cloth dipped in glue to give a painting surface. A glaze may be applied after to give a sheen to the creature. Details like the eyes are beads glued to thin wire embedded in the body.

The advantage of polystyrene is that it can be carved quickly with little practice. In the case of the fruit, different shapes are coated with cloth or papier mâché and fixed to wire which is then taped on to a branch. A cloth or papier mâché surface not only allows painting but other things to be glued on to the form such as felt and paper skins, leaves and textures.

The cross is a simple carving exercise but it can be elaborated upon after covering with papier mâché or gauze dipped in glue. This is illustrated by the bas relief carving of the knight and dragon in which papier mâché, felt and string can work up the detail to a great delicacy.

The angel, if not carved from a solid block, can be made up of many pieces of polystyrene, wired and glued together into the rough form and then cut into the finished shape by a hot knife or wire tool. The wings or even the arms may be made by taped wire forms inserted deep into the polystyrene body. A surface or papier mâché or paper, canvas or gauze soaked in hot size should help to secure the two materials to each other. The wings can be finished by cutting out felt feathers and gluing them over the papier mâché form of wire. Shellac or glue will stiffen the felt and make it ready for painting or gilding. If the figure requires drapery this can be obtained by dipping canvas into hot size or sculptor's scrim into plaster and draping it carefully before it hardens.

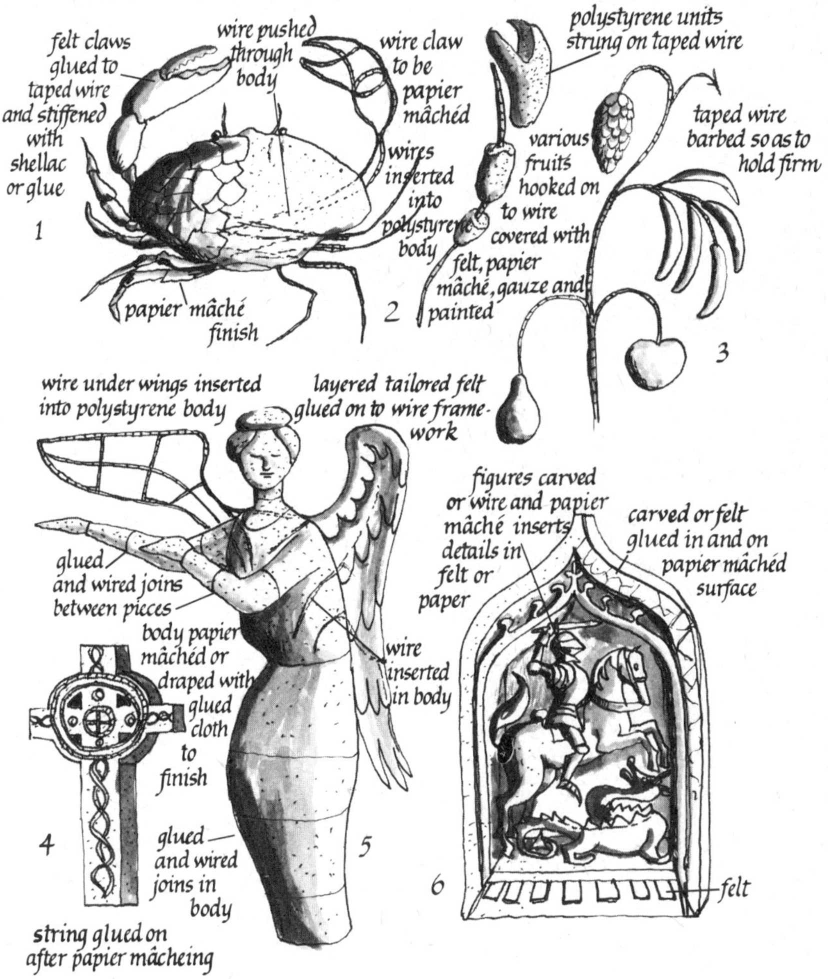

FIGURE 58

1, 2. Crab
3. Fruit
4. Cross
5. Angel
6. Bas relief

FIBREGLASS is a tough, light plastic made up of a cold-setting polyester resin reinforced with glass fibre. It is principally used in prop making for casting and replication in quantity, although it may be used in one-off jobs. The resin, a syrupy substance, is made hard by adding a chemical catalyst. This process can take from 30 minutes upwards depending on room temperature and the chemical accelerator present in the mix. During the transition from liquid through the gelatine stage to the solid state, called the "working time", it is combined with a filler or colour and glass fibre layers so as eventually to form a hard skin of desired thickness. The resin usually comes in cans ranging from ½ pint to a gallon. The catalyst comes in smaller quantities and the manufacturers' recommended proportion of catalyst to resin should be mutually mixed in a separate container, never in the resin can. Use the minimum amount needed for each stage.

The task of chemical separators, whether they be wax, emulsion or alcohol based, is to act as a barrier between the mould and the cast. This is necessary because resin is a powerful adhesive. The function of fillers can be to stiffen the surface coat of a job and give it an opaque body or carry a desired pigment colour. This includes metallic fillers which not only stiffen the resin but give it a polishable surface and thus the illusion of a solid metallic cast. Methylated spirit is used to clean the stiff brush used to work resin and fibre together.

There are several types of glass fibre: chopped strand mat of various weights is a good general purpose material; cloth is stronger but more expensive; and scrim is a useful open weave where one needs a thicker laminate or layer than cloth, but less than mat.

Warning. Working with resin and glass can be a mild health hazard, so purchase a recommended barrier cream and wear long sleeved and tight clothes. Beware also of glass dust when sand-papering and never have a naked light nearby.

Vinyl

Vinyl is a rubbery plastic that is melted in an air crucible and used for mould material. It is bought in slabs, cut into little pieces and slowly melted in a sealed crucible before being poured into a retaining reservoir containing the object to be replicated. Let it cool and harden in its own time.

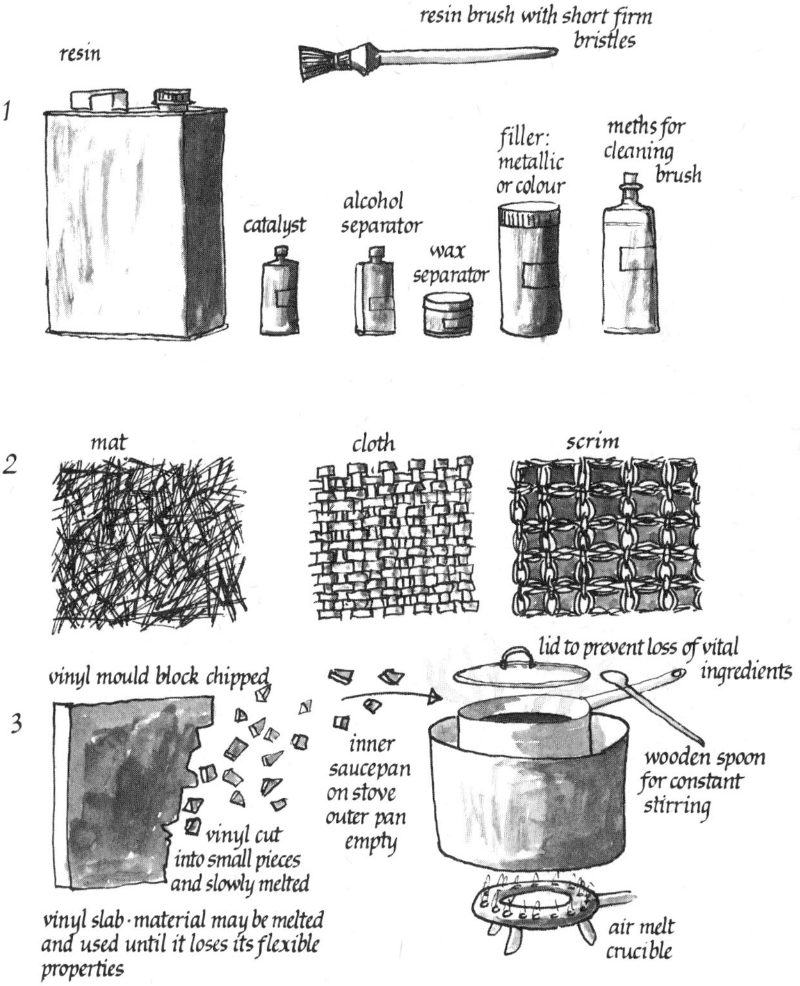

FIGURE 59

1. Fibreglass materials
2. Types of glass fibre
3. Working with vinyl

FIBREGLASS: TWO-PIECE PLASTER MOULD

A HEAD or object is made on an armature of wood and wire from clay or Plasticine. It is then divided into fore and aft by a fence made up of foil plates (these can be made of cut-up tin cans). A zig-zag pattern is lined down the long side to act as a key when the join has to be matched on the mould. The head is then lightly greased with petroleum jelly or oil which is to act as a separator to the plaster; the latter is initially flicked on to the model after being mixed to the correct consistency with water. Slowly, as it hardens, more and more plaster is applied, until the head is completely buried, except for the plate fence of which just the tip should be left. When the plaster is dry and brittle the mould should be broken open by pulling out the plates. The two halves should come apart easily and the original is then extracted. After cleaning out the interior of the mould it should be treated with a wax separator.

The first layer of catalysed resin is brushed into every cranny. This is called the "gelcoat" and may be filled with colour, metal or just opaque fillers if a translucency is not needed. When the gelcoat becomes tacky, brush on a further coat of resin and add the first mat layer. This is dabbed into position with a stiff brush. In time, with the jabbing motion, the glass fibre will eventually merge with the hardened resin to form a glassy mass. Eliminate all bubbles. When the texture of the fibre disappears, allow to harden before applying the next layer. Cut up the glass mat and after priming the surface with resin repeat process, dabbing the fibres with a resin-soaked brush. Eliminate all strands that stick up and apply the third laminate when ready. Allow to "cure" before removing from mould. After extracting carefully from the half mould, cut edges with fine saw, file and sandpaper. Then butt edges together and laminate join on the inside. This may be done in or out of the mould as long as the two halves are secured. The outer joints are treated with pure or filled resin and sandpapered flush to desired surface. If further colouring is required a fine sandpapered surface will allow a paint to key on to it.

The same plaster mould may be used for a plaster head. This is useful for statues or objects that have to be broken every night. A thin-shelled, and therefore easily breakable model is obtained by pouring plaster into a wire-secured and upturned two-piece mould and swilling it about until it sets.

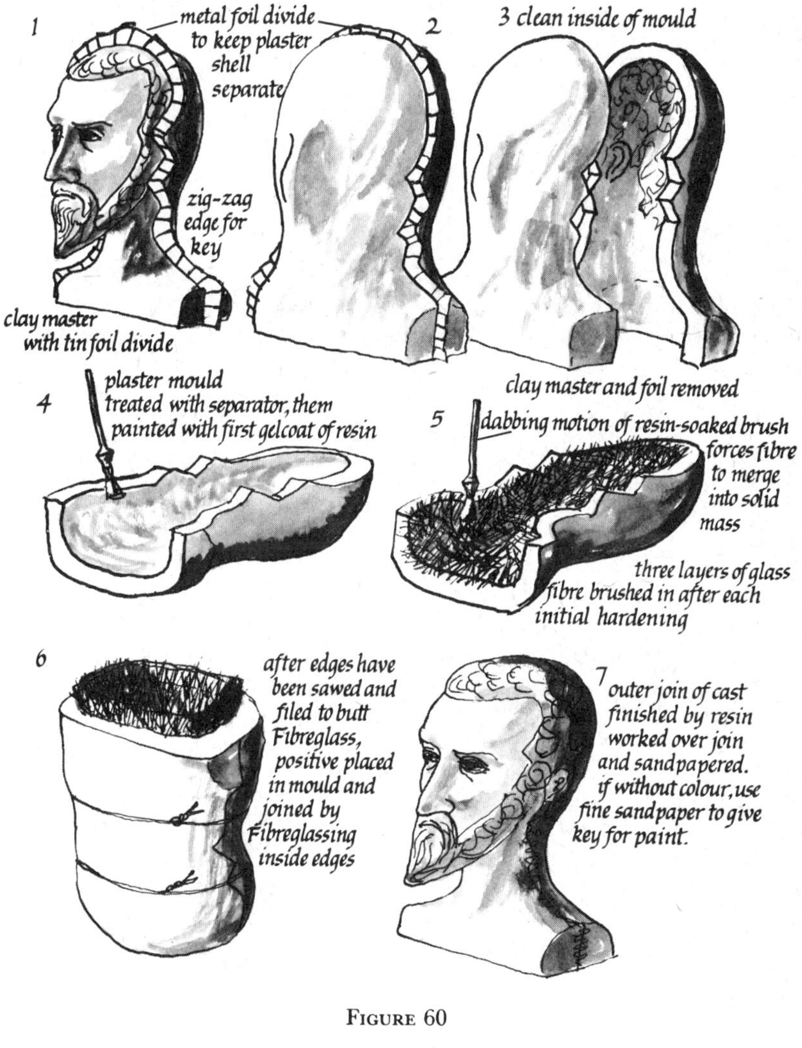
1
metal foil divide to keep plaster shell separate
2
3 clean inside of mould
zig-zag edge for key
clay master with tin foil divide
clay master and foil removed
4
plaster mould treated with separator, them painted with first gelcoat of resin
5
dabbing motion of resin-soaked brush forces fibre to merge into solid mass
three layers of glass fibre brushed in after each initial hardening
6
after edges have been sawed and filed to butt Fibreglass, positive placed in mould and joined by Fibreglassing inside edges
7
outer join of cast finished by resin worked over join and sandpapered. if without colour, use fine sandpaper to give key for paint.

FIGURE 60

FIBREGLASS AND VINYL MOULD

THE original object may be made of wood, plaster, Plasticine, clay, metal or even glass or china. It can be fairly detailed and full of deep undercuts. If the object to be cast is porous, it must be treated so as to avoid penetration by hot vinyl. This sealing can be done by three coats of shellac, three coats of aluminium paint and a last one of shellac. Objects such as glass and china need to be heated before the hot vinyl is poured over them or they will crack.

The simple mould illustrated is made up either of an old tin or a cylinder of metal foil, embedded in a clay base and sealed with tape and wire. The object is then placed inside and secured or weighted so as to prevent it floating up in the hot vinyl. The vinyl, prepared by slowly melting small pieces in an air crucible, is then poured into the container and allowed to cool in its own time. When it is hard, the mould is extracted from the reservoir and slit open to release the original. The slightly greasy and flexible mould can then be put to use by applying the Fibreglass processes of gelcoat and successive layers of matted glass pressed into catalysed resin. In the case of the goblet, the technique is applied first to the open mould halves, which are then closed and secured by tape or twisted wire, and worked on by poking resin and glass down the stem and into and round the bowl. The stem could be further reinforced by inserting wire from base to bowl. If weight is needed in the bottom, metallic powder or a nut or bolt could be incorporated in the base. Colour or metal can be introduced at the gelcoat stage or it could be left as translucent. A high polish can be obtained by metal polish after the edges have been sawed or filed trim and after an initial fine sandpapering.

The vinyl mould can be used for many copies and is useful for replicating such objects as knives, statues and pistols. For larger objects, a more complex procedure is needed which requires a plaster case containing the vinyl mould proper. This is obtained by surrounding the object with a clay envelope and covering this with plaster. When the plaster is dry the clay is taken out, leaving a void between the plaster and the model which is then filled with vinyl. When the original is removed we have a strong case supporting a flexible vinyl mould which is then filled with Fibreglass or plaster in the usual way.

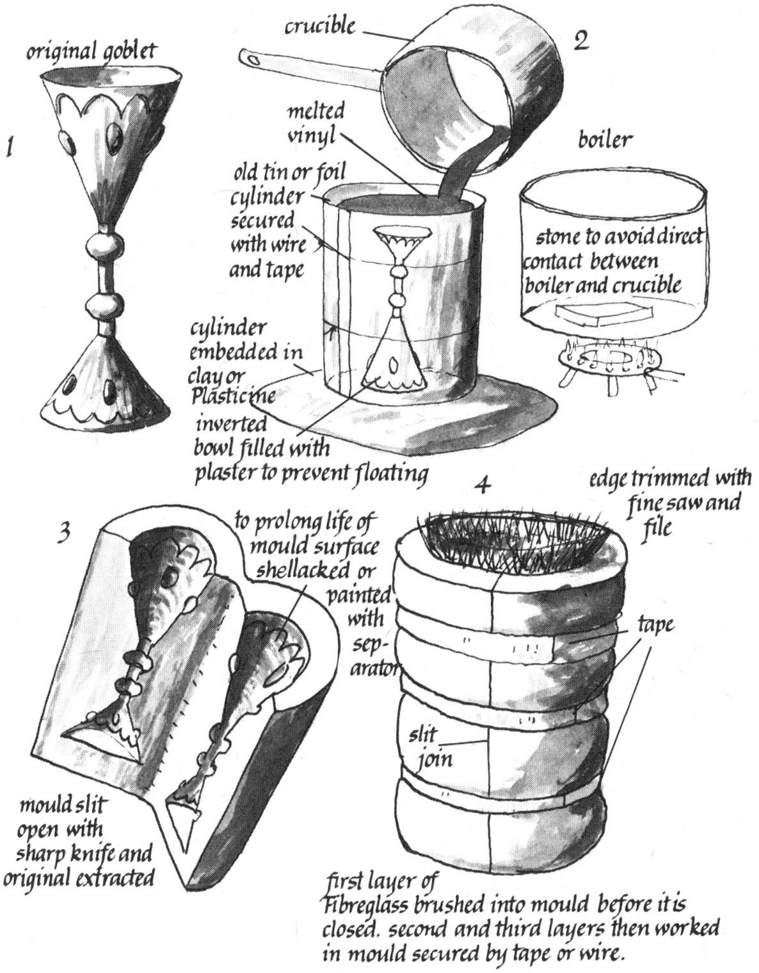
original goblet
1
crucible
2
melted
vinyl
boiler
old tin or foil
cylinder
secured
with wire
and tape
stone to avoid direct
contact between
boiler and crucible
cylinder
embedded in
clay or
Plasticine
inverted
bowl filled with
plaster to prevent floating
4
edge trimmed with
fine saw and
file
3
to prolong life of
mould surface
shellacked or
painted
with
sep-
arator
tape
slit
join
mould slit
open with
sharp knife and
original extracted
first layer of
Fibreglass brushed into mould before it is
closed. second and third layers then worked
in mould secured by tape or wire.

Figure 61

DOCUMENTS, BOOKS AND CHARTS

To make parchment-like paper, take a fair quality sheet of cartridge paper and paint it with shellac on both sides after writing in the text with waterproof indian ink. This will give it the slightly brittle quality and colour. Colour may also be obtained by painting the paper with (unmilked) tea. To fold correctly, fold all four sides into the centre, then fold once more to envelop edges. Pierce with a knife, insert red ribbon, wrap around twice and seal with sealing wax stamped with symbol, which can be made from a linocut.

Up to about the year 1800 horoscopes were drawn out in the format illustrated. They varied in size, but one foot square is about right. The paper may be treated as described above to give a parchment effect. Below are the planetary and zodiacal symbols used.

To make an ancient or ornamental book, take an old and substantial volume like a Victorian encyclopaedia and glue the appropriate material, such as leather or rough paper, to its spine and covers. The raised ribs of the spine can be made of rope and the ridges along the edges of string or braid glued on the painted or papier mâchéd cover. Real or paper lace, such as that used for table mats, can be glued on to give intricate textures. Card or felt shapes or papier mâché figures may be fixed into a design. Jewels are made up of either stage jewels or cheap fragments or composed of fruit gums, clear or coloured boiled sweets, cotton wool or bits of polystyrene set beneath coloured transparent paper glued into position. Metallic foil paper can be used to good effect as can any gilded string or thread.

Hanging maps or charts can be made of shellac-treated cartridge paper or canvas primed with white paint. After the drawing is complete, the chart is fixed with drawing pins or tacks to two wooden rods or dowelling which serve as rollers when the map is not in use. Ribbon on the top rod serves as a hanger and below as the securer. Ageing of maps is done with shellac or (unmilked) tea.

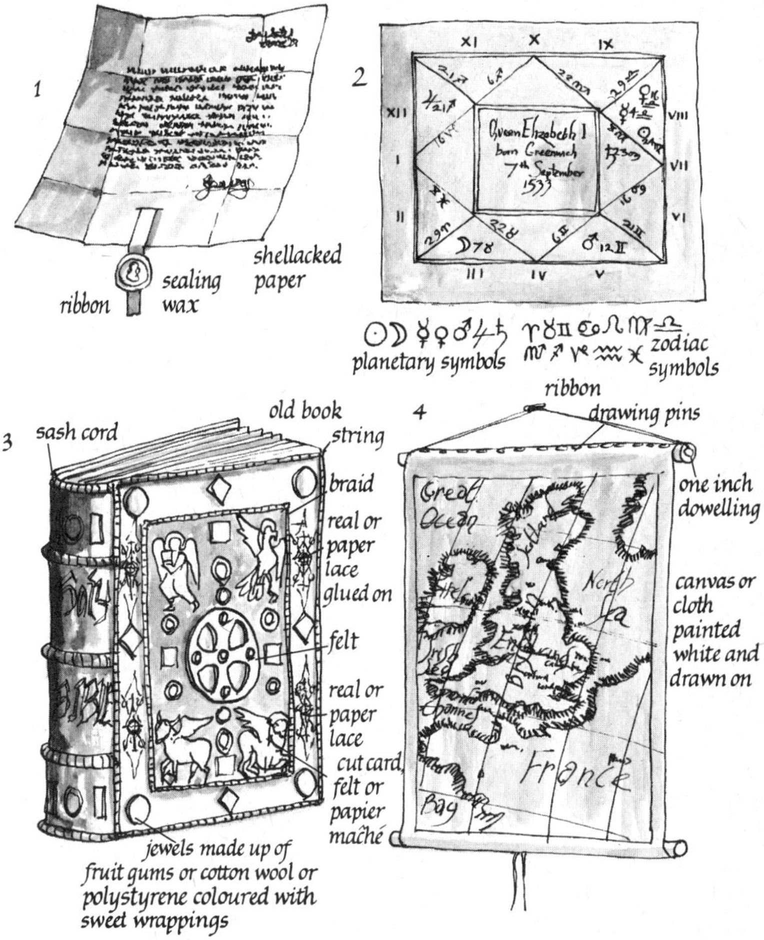

FIGURE 62

1. Parchment
2. Horoscope
3. Ornamental book
4. Hanging map

PRACTICAL CLOCK, STAINED GLASS AND SPECTACLES

A CLOCK that moves on stage to show the passage of time is a prop-effect device. It can be made from an existing clock on the principle illustrated here. The method is based on a hollow tube with a rod or wire down the middle. The existing or specially-made hour hand of card, felt or wood is fixed to the tube by glue, while the minute hand is simply made by bending the wire or rod at right angles to the turning axis and gluing on an arrowhead end. The twin-turning axis passes through the clock, now empty of works, and comes out at the back in a corresponding mirror position so that when turned in the opposite direction the front face hands turn in the clockwise motion. Make an anti-clockwise face and practise the hour and minute hand speeds to get the right ratio of movement. With the front well decorated, the back of the mechanism can be operated from behind the stage flat.

Stained glass may be made up of a transparent plastic sheet such as Cinemoid or Cellophane set in a wooden frame and lightly sand-papered to give a key for the coloured inks or french enamel varnishes to be used. The leading can either be painted in heavy black or laid out in black masking tape. Any fine drawing should be done with coloured indian inks.

Both spectacles and lorgnette are made of wire and tape. Many shapes and sizes can be made by this method with as much added decoration as is needed, with shellac or glue-stiffened felt or card, stage jewellery and braid as the objects will require. A clear or tinted transparent plastic can easily be taped into the frames. With skill, a high level of delicacy can be obtained.

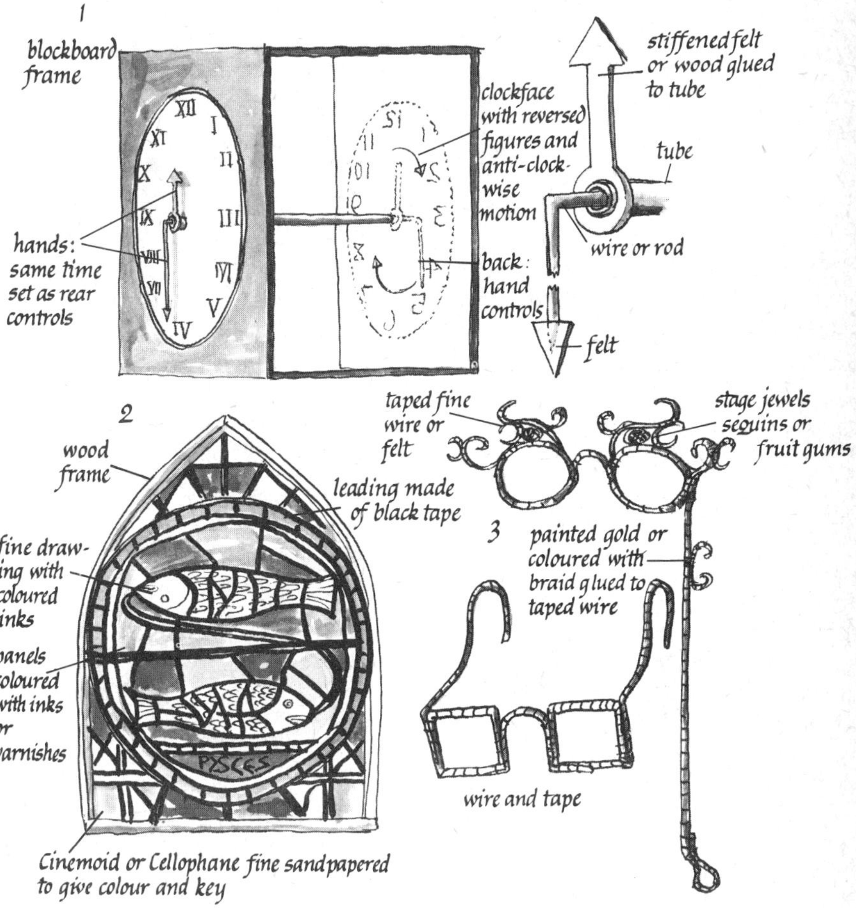

FIGURE 63

1. Practical clock
2. Stained glass window
3. Spectacles

ASTROLOGERS' TOOLS

An armillary sphere was part of an astrologer's equipment. To make one, build a wire and tape frame base and glue round and over it thick card or skin ply. The tiny earth globe at the centre is a small rubber ball. The whole is weighted at the base by burying beneath the papier mâché foot a load of old nuts and bolts. The angel is made up of fuse wire and tape and then papier mâchéd. Paint the whole piece black, then paint or spray it gold or bronze. The inside of the zodiac band could be painted blue with the sun and moon, cut from card, glued in after. Draw the calibration and the zodiac signs and symbols in indian ink. String decoration and some Latin quotation should finish the job.

A telescope may be made up of paper tubes covered with brass foil paper or painted gold. The tubes are fixed into each other by glue and tape to make a stiff fit, if needed, in the base of the larger tubes. The joins can be finished off with glued braid and the glass at each end made up of old lenses or transparent plastic. The symbols can be drawn on the side. The clamp device to hold the telescope is made from a wooden disc with a nut and bolt axis that allows the telescope to elevate or depress. The telescope is held in position by broom-handle clips screwed into the disc. The support column is made of wood, wire, tape, string, and papier mâché decoration. It is a thick dowel set into a wooden base.

The crystal ball is made from the top part of a large electric bulb, filled with hardened clear fibreglass resin. It is set in a wooden base and decorated with braid, string, paper rope, and paint.

The astrolabe was another vital tool for the old astrologers. Here a replica is made up of a wooden base and carefully cut out card or felt. If gold foil card can be obtained, this could be used for the intricate facing and the surface of the main plate. A central nut should be inserted for accuracy, with a holding ring for handling. The size of the instrument varied from six inches to one foot in diameter.

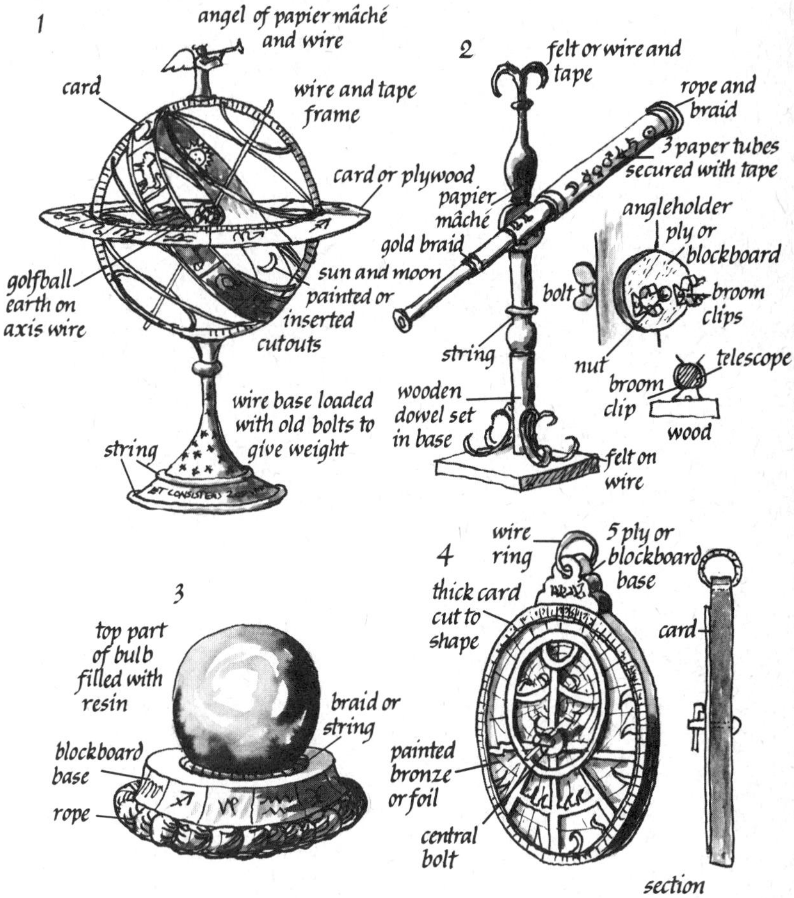

FIGURE 64

1. Armillary sphere
2. Telescope
3. Crystal ball
4. Astrolabe

HOOK AND FLUFF FASTENER (VELCRO)

MADE out of minute plastic hooks and fluff, the fastening material known in England as Velcro, is extremely useful in prop making. It is made in different colours and in strips and patches, and is composed of two elements which when pressed together make a firm hold on one another until, with a moderate pull, they are parted. The principle is the gripping action of the tiny hooks on the fine plastic fluff. As a plastic material Velcro may be sewn or glued or pinned or nailed to most surfaces. The illustrations depict some of its uses.

In the goose leg the Velcro is glued to the papier mâché body and leg so that it may be ripped off, with realistic noise, and replaced for the next show. On the costume we see its use for quickly fastening cloaks, badges and insignia which may be rapidly interchanged with others should the same costume be used for other situations. On the book, Velcro can be used for a fastening. It could be used in a similar manner on a purse or any prop needing this kind of reliable and easy fastening. A button or stud may be glued over the Velcro strip to give the illusion of a conventional fastening. The same technique is applied to stage jewellery, as seen in the bracelet. This method can mean that jewellery or ornamentation can be adhered to Velcro-prepared costumes, props or scenery for rapid setting and striking. In the last illustration, Velcro is seen to be used to its full convenience. Here spring, summer and autumn leaves can be put on and taken off in easy sequence. Likewise with fruit, flowers and additional growth or decay as the play progresses. Such objects as the butterfly are easily set and removed if the site and the insect, made of thin wire and gauze, have a small piece of the hook and fluff fastening glued or sewn to them.

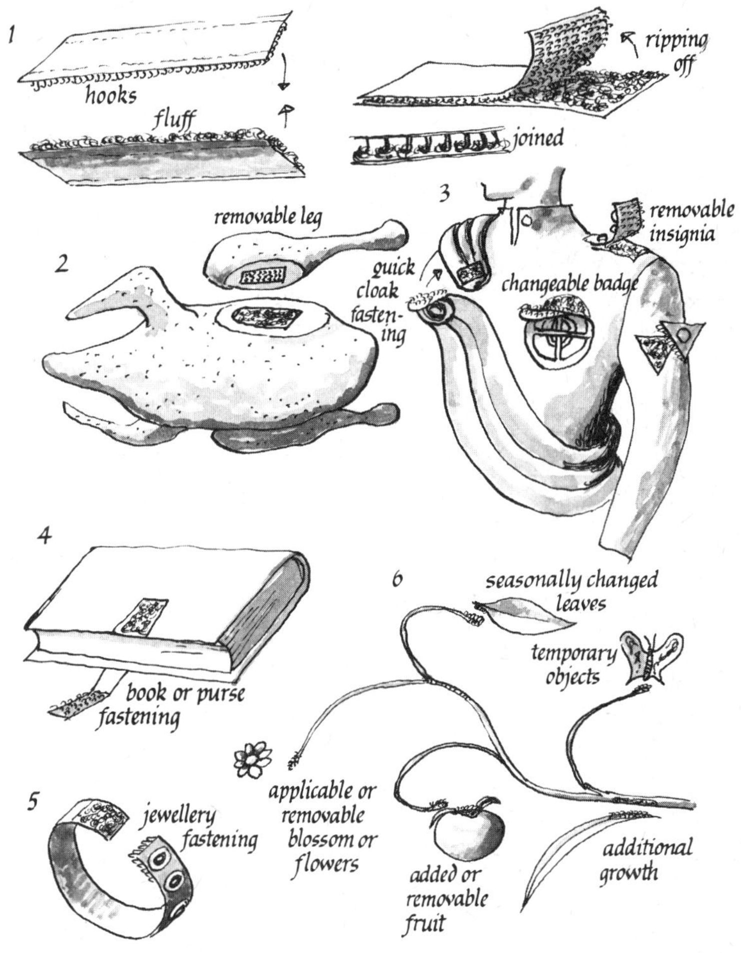

FIGURE 65

1. Velcro principle
2–6. Examples

ROPES, CORDS AND STRINGS

THERE are many different kinds of ropes, cords and strings, ranging from very thick to very thin, which have a variety of uses in prop making. They can be made of natural fibres, paper, plastic or metallic threads. All have their uses. Here is a selection.

Paper rope, which comes in very wide or moderately thin thicknesses, can be used simply as decoration, such as winding round a column, at the base and top of objects, or as a flexible material suitable for the snake with the felt head glued on to it. It can also be used to line a decorative border, like the sash cord in the third illustration, or papier-mâchéd over to make a high ridge round the edge of objects (*see* censer). With ordinary rope, this same technique can be applied according to the size required. However, conventional rope has another advantage in that it can be broken down into small strings that have a useful curly characteristic. Taken further it can be finely shredded so as to make hair for props or makeup. This latter use is applied by gluing the unbound strands with a rubber-based glue to a piece of gauze shaped to the face or glued to a cap for a wig (*see* fig. 45). The second illustration here shows the possibilities for braiding beards, moustaches and eyebrows. More formalised hair, such as that used on sculpture, is achieved by simply gluing many fine lengths of string on to the object, then hardening the desired set by soaking it in hot size or water paste. Shellac may also be used. It can then be painted in stone, wood or metallic colours to give the illusion of carving. The same technique is used in the knife, but with an eye for decoration. This decorative use of strings and cords combined with felt and paper sculpture can be quite elaborate. The tassel illustrates the various uses of paper rope, glued cord and shredded string. Gold braids may be exploited in a similar way.

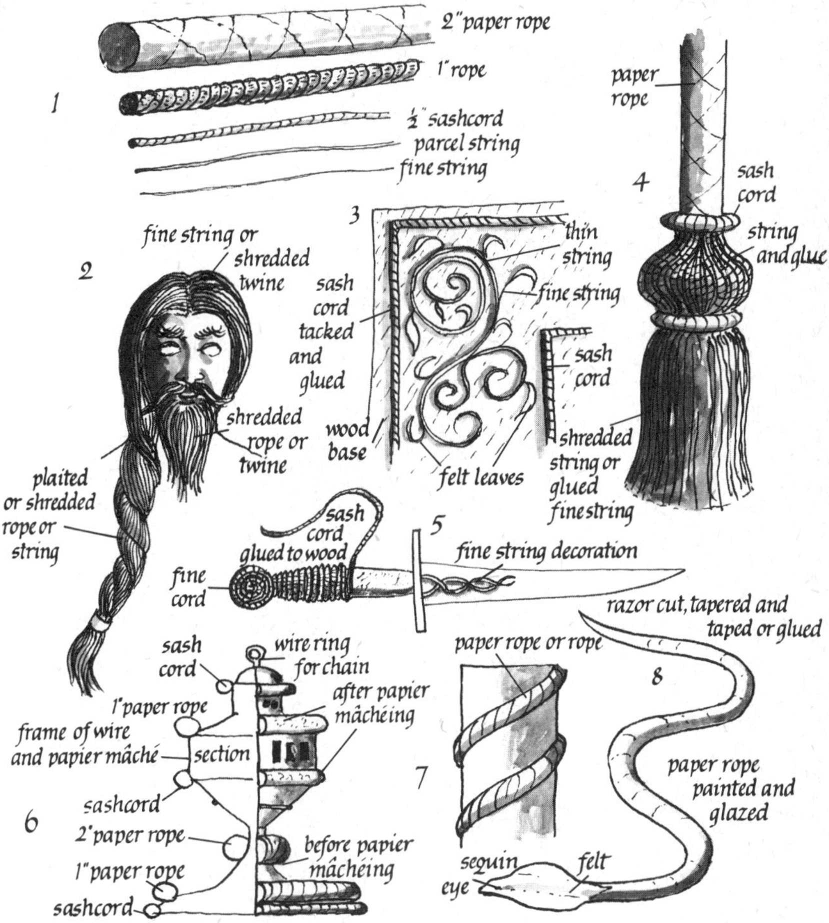

FIGURE 66

1. Ropes and cord
2. Rope for hair
3. Relief decoration
4. Tassel
5. Knife
6. Censer
7. Carving
8. Snake

CHURCH OBJECTS, MIRROR AND MINIATURE

THE key is made from a piece of wooden dowel with a drilled and sawn piece of wood glued to one end. The other end is made up of taped wire with felt or card glued into decorative patterns, the whole stiffened with shellac or glue. String is glued round the barrel of the key.

The miniature is based on an oval of plywood with a reproduction cut from a book glued to it. This is covered with a clear book-cover laminate or something like the Cellophane that wraps cigarette packets. The edge has gold braid glued round it.

The cross is of wood, with a wire and papier mâché figure stapled to it. The ends are of card, tape and wire, the insets drawn and filled with paper lace and made-up jewellery.

The monstrance is made up of a wooden base and a central column of dowelling (broom handle) surmounted by a wire ring, with details in fine wire, felt, card, string and braid. The transparent element is made of clear plastic. The mirror is treated in a similar way, with an old glass fixed to a wooden handle, then decorated with taped wire, felt and card stiffened with shellac, hot size or water paste. The whole is painted according to requirements. After papier-mâchéing, stage jewels (*see* fig. 17) can be set into the borders.

The relic box is composed of three pieces of wood taped together with cloth tape for hinges. It can be decorated with velvet, drawing pins and silver paper lace. It is fastened by hook and fluff material.

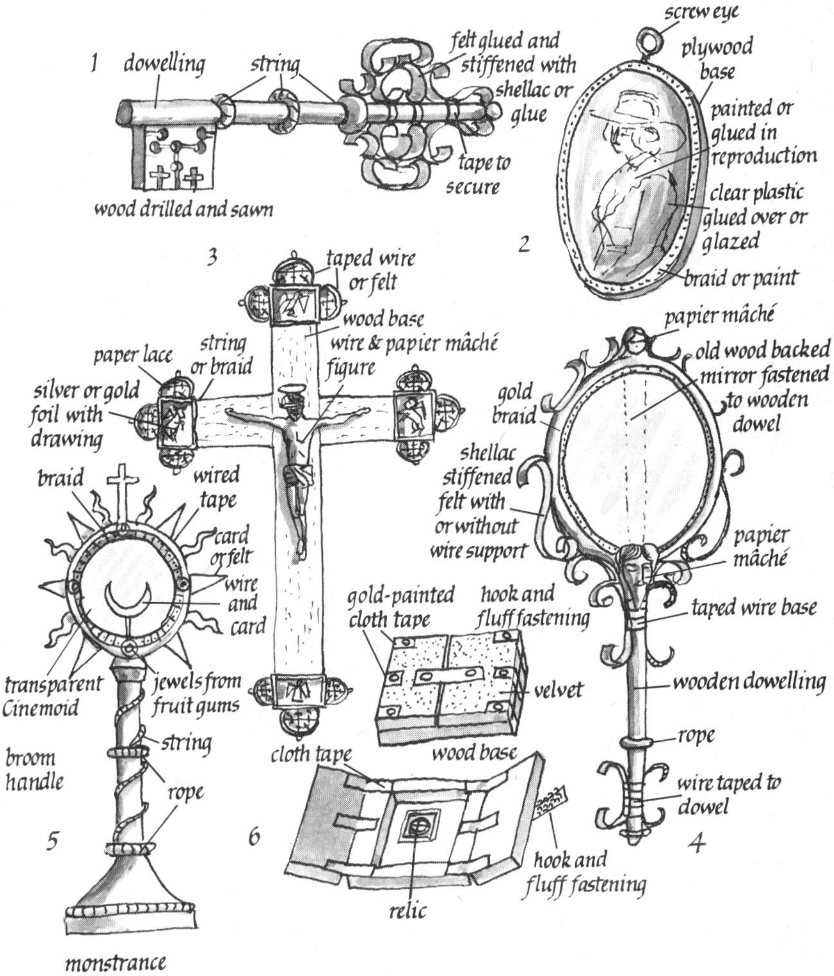

Figure 67

1. Key
2. Miniature
3. Cross
4. Mirror
5. Monstrance
6. Reliquary

PAPER LACE

PAPER replicas of real lace are used as table mats in the home to protect polished surfaces from coffee and cakes. In propmaking these quite detailed reproductions can be put to good use in various ways. The sword in our second illustration shows how paper lace can be glued round the hilt to make a fine chiselled steel filigree. It may also, when cut into smaller units, be applied to the blade, wrist guard and pommel of the weapon. Some paper lace mat patterns actually come in gold or silver so that they need not be painted black, then dry-brushed in metallic paints. The paper lace, if not stiffened by the paint, can be treated with shellac, paper paste or hot size.

To make the plate shown opposite, paper lace is glued to a plate's centre and smaller units to the edge. This, when painted, will give a unified impression of a finely moulded or engraved piece of metal or china. The base plate may be of metal, plastic or the real thing.

The goblet illustrated could be of metal or glass with carefully tailored pieces of paper lace glued round its bowl, stem and base— the rest left or painted to match. The same technique is applied to the knife, with the lace (real or paper) glued to the leather or wood, then brushed with metallic paint.

Paper lace can be used for costume collars and cuffs. First cut, then glued into the right shapes, they make good imitations of the real thing.

The last illustration shows how an object may be decorated with white lace on black or black lace on white to give an ivory effect. There are many applications for this material to make things ornate. One example is that it may be used as a stencil to make regular and elegant wall or fabric patterns (*see* fig. 53).

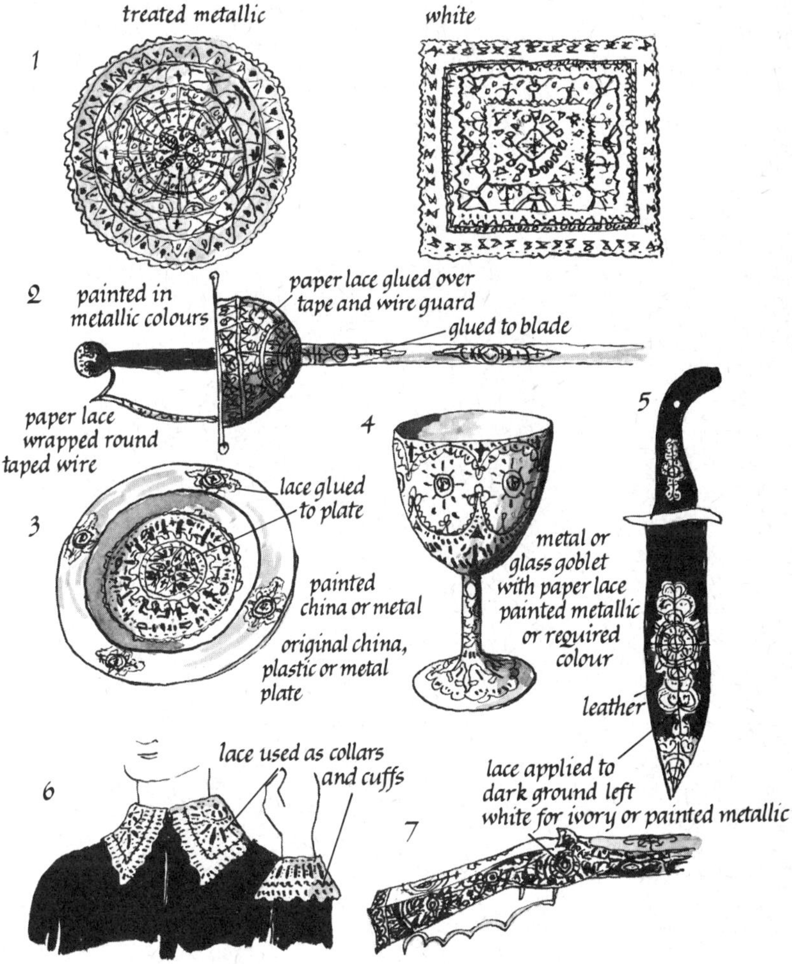

FIGURE 68

1. Examples of paper lace
2. Sword
3. Plate
4. Goblet
5. Knife
6. Collar and cuff
7. Ivory effect

LETTERING

THE use of lettering and various scripts occurs constantly in propmaking. So it is useful to know their style and period if only to know where to search for a sample of a period. On the opposite page is a selection ranging from celtic script through the mediaeval to the renaissance. Also included are some illuminated letters and monograms. By thoughtfully studying a small sample one could even, if one did not have the full alphabet, fake up the style of a manuscript by copying the graphic characteristics of the given letter. This is the art of the propmaker.

ABC
10th cent
ABC
14th cent
abc
14th cent
14th cent
9th cent
16th cent
Elizabethan monogram
Christian monogram
16th cent
ABC
Gothic
Italique hande
Italic 16th - 17th cent

FIGURE 69

PLASTICS, PRACTICAL KNIFE AND CHAINS

LATEX foam rubber is a very useful material for other things besides cushioning. It can be used, as shown here, for the spikes of the morning star club where sharp cones are glued to a rubber or polystyrene ball. The chain joining the papier-mâchéd sphere to the stick can be made of real chain or rope woven to look like chain, then stiffened by size or shellac. The whole weapon is painted black, then dry brushed with silver. The cane chain is made of cane bent over a flame or electric stove and taped into links. Quite large chains can be made in this way.

The practical knife is a simple spring-loaded device made from a flattened tube and blade. After the mechanism has been perfected it can be decorated in the usual manner. The securing neck unit will need some delicate workmanship but it is not beyond a fair craftsman. Make sure it is not used too often or too vigorously.

Polystyrene broken up into fine pieces makes good snow or hail, though it clings annoyingly. Another use for foam rubber or plastic sponge is seen in the flexible fish. Here the basic shape is sculpted then covered with iridescent gauze to give it a sheen. If this is not obtainable glitter can be sprinkled on the body, lightly touched with glue. The fins and tail are made of thin wires inserted through the body and covered with gauze or some semi-transparent material. The eyes are glass beads or sequins.

Many plastic shapes are to be found in the home. These may be used to form the basis for props ranging from delicate jewellery to architectural forms. After selecting the right size and shape, the plastic is pierced with wire, taped and covered in papier mâché, or draped with glued or shellacked cloth. The illustration gives some idea of the variety to be utilised. All are good starting points for a particular job.

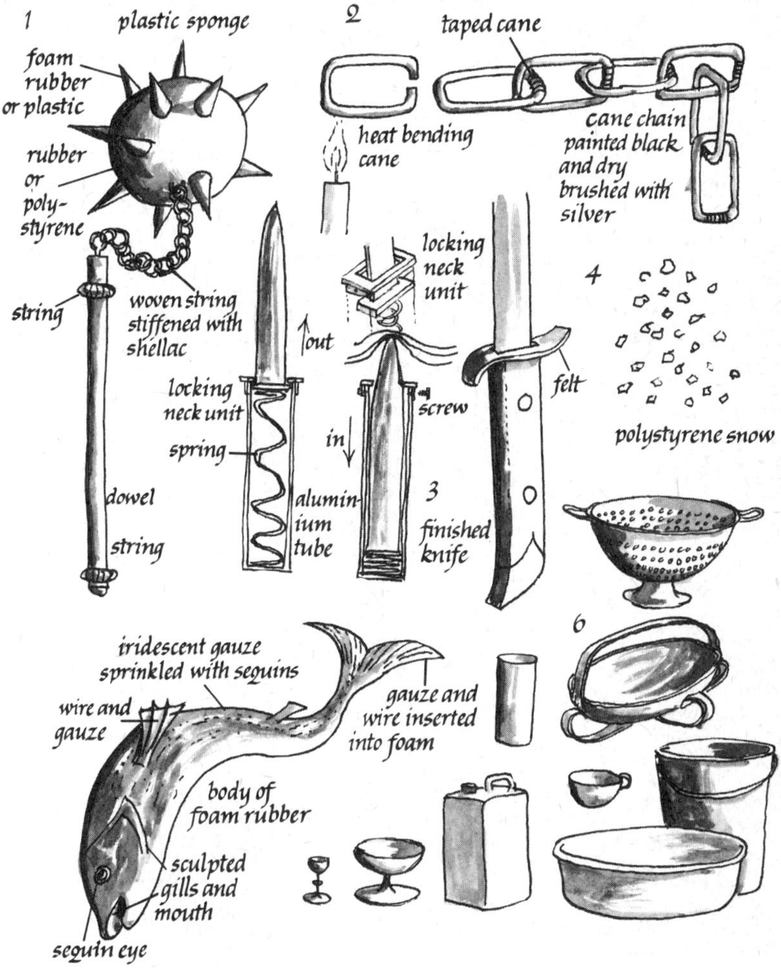

Figure 70

1. Morning star
2. Chain
3. Practical knife
4. Snow
5. Fish
6. Plastic shapes

LATEX AND RUBBER GLUES

THERE is now available a rubber-based moulding and casting material that goes hard either by adding a catalyst or simply by contact with air. This substance has advantages and disadvantages. The main disadvantage is high cost. Illustrated are some applications to exploit its characteristics. The first is to make a lifelike hand. Here a clay bath if set up with a person's hand, after greasing, placed on a slight mould to stop the hand flattening. Plaster is then flicked on to the top side of the hand until it is covered. When it is just beyond the hardened stage the whole complex should be reversed and the hand extracted. This will give a half mould, as seen in the second illustration, with keyholes to match the top mould when it is made. This is done after the first mould has been shellacked and greased and the hand replaced in the negative hollow again, but palm up. The hand is then flicked with plaster again and removed when the plaster is just past the hardened stage. The shellacked and greased surface of the mould should bring easy separation and also allow, with keys, for the two moulds to be united accurately, ready for pouring in the latex. Depending on temperature, the latex hardens at its surfaces from 20 minutes to several hours. The trick, however, is to pour out the latex at the right moment, which may or may not involve a catalyst (check manufacturer's instructions), leaving a skin form which can then be pulled out of the mould. If it needs to be solid, the glove-like cast can be filled with foam rubber or plastic sponge.

The same principle of casting is applied to the full head mask except that the original is based on a clay master sculptured and plaster moulded in the conventional way (*see* fig. 59). In this case the mould is filled with air-hardening latex which is then poured back into the can when a skin has been formed on the mould's surface. A cheaper method but one that requires great patience is to use a small amount of latex and gently swill it round the mould until it hardens. Here one needs a chemically accelerated latex. When the cast is pulled out, the mouth and eye holes are cut out and edge-trimmed. The same technique is applied to the breastplate which can be made by a paste-type latex smoothed into a prepared mould. The latex is painted when fully cured.

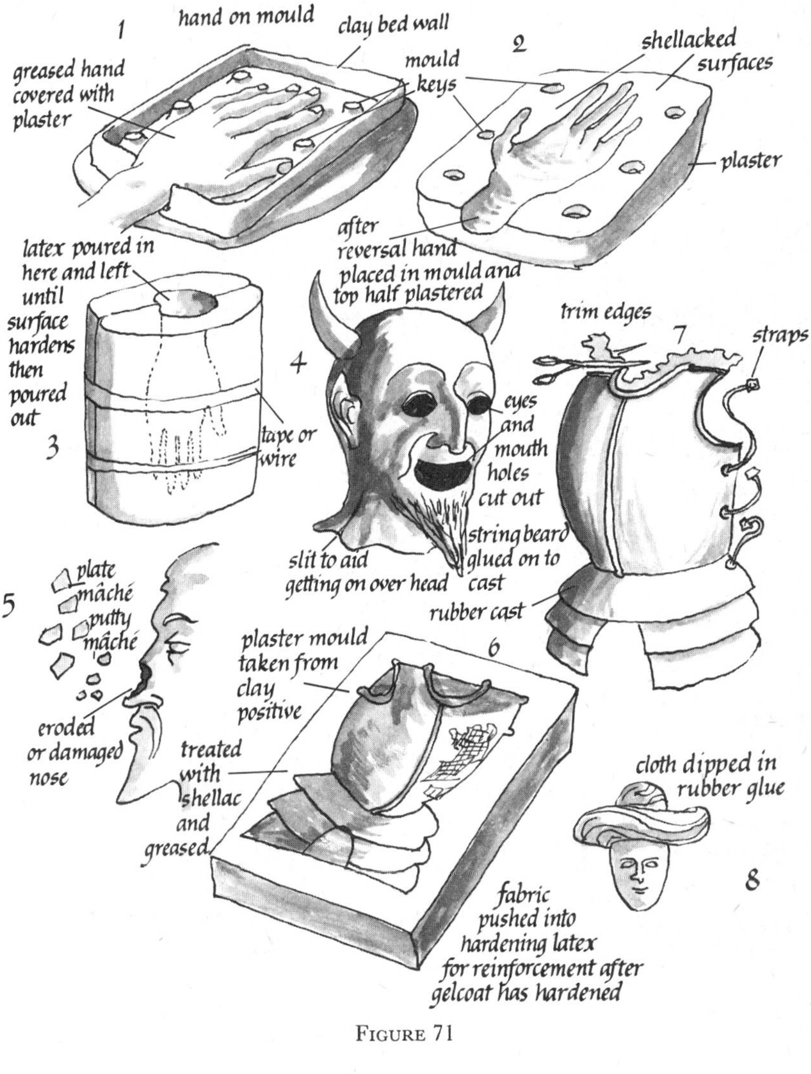
1
hand on mould
clay bed wall
greased hand covered with plaster
mould keys
2
shellacked surfaces
plaster
after reversal hand placed in mould and top half plastered
latex poured in here and left until surface hardens then poured out
tape or wire
3
4
eyes and mouth holes cut out
string beard glued on to cast
slit to aid getting on over head
trim edges
7
straps
rubber cast
5
plate mâché
putty mâché
eroded or damaged nose
plaster mould taken from clay positive
6
treated with shellac and greased
cloth dipped in rubber glue
8
fabric pushed into hardening latex for reinforcement after gelcoat has hardened

FIGURE 71

COAT OF ARMS

In this example a multiple of techniques is used. First a wooden base is made to which taped wire and wood shapes are fixed. Slowly the detail is built up. The crown is made of velvet with metallic card or foil glued to wire forms. Stage jewels complete it. The helmet is based on a carved polystyrene block set in the central column by being spiked and glued. It is then papier-mâchéd and decorated with card or stiffened felt. The surrounding drapes are glued felt or cloth, supported by taped wire affixed to the main frame. The motto is card, cut and bent to shape with painted or cutout lettering glued on. The halberds and flags are of dowelling, card or felt and cloth, soaked in hot glue, shellac or paste. The shield is made up of wood, string, braid, felt and painted shapes. The lion is a semi-solid papier mâché figure with string or felt to finish, while the dragon is a relief made up of cutout paper or felt scales glued to a slightly curved surface of papier mâché. The details are of wire, string, sequins and paint. The lower drapes are stiffened canvas or felt glued to wire and tape supports, with the swords of wood, card, felt and string. The medallion is a wooden block, with string or braid and papier mâché. The decorative leaves are of taped wire and felt or leather leaves with the fruit made of papier-mâchéd polystyrene. The whole could be painted as stone, wood or metal and suspended by a strong hook screwed into the back of the wooden frame.

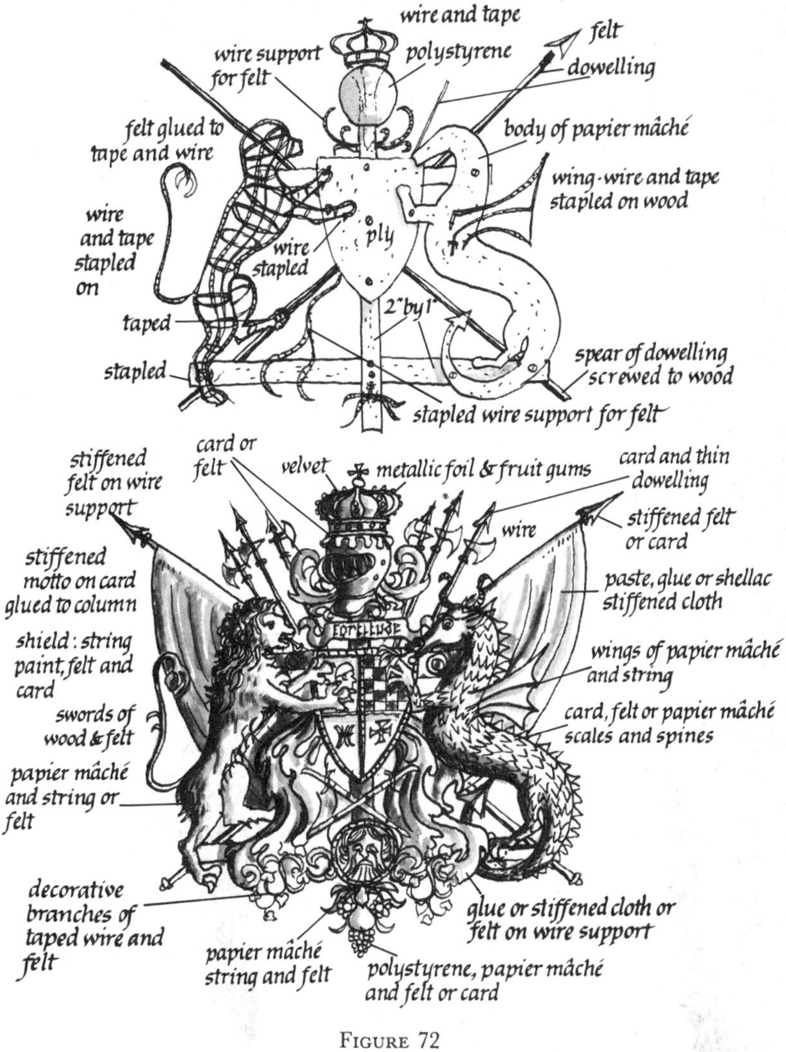
wire and tape
felt
wire support for felt
polystyrene
dowelling
felt glued to tape and wire
body of papier mâché
wing-wire and tape stapled on wood
wire and tape stapled on
wire stapled
ply
taped
2" by 1"
stapled
spear of dowelling screwed to wood
stapled wire support for felt
stiffened felt on wire support
card or felt
velvet
metallic foil & fruit gums
card and thin dowelling
wire
stiffened felt or card
stiffened motto on card glued to column
paste, glue or shellac stiffened cloth
shield: string paint, felt and card
wings of papier mâché and string
swords of wood & felt
card, felt or papier mâché scales and spines
papier mâché and string or felt
decorative branches of taped wire and felt
glue or stiffened cloth or felt on wire support
papier mâché string and felt
polystyrene, papier mâché and felt or card

FIGURE 72